**Dedicated to
Clinton Hawkins,
great student
and friend.**

Trafford PUBLISHING®   www.trafford.com

North America & international
toll-free: 844-688-6899 (USA & Canada)
fax: 812 355 4082

For more information, see the following websites:
www.angelfire.com/al/ellisaikido/
www.geocities.com/ellisaikido/
www.geocities.com/britishaikido

This book is a solid and practical look into 45 years of traditional training and teaching. The authors don't pretend to understand all there is to know about such a complex martial art as Aikido, nor do they wish to create the impression that they have the answers to the many questions being raised within the Aikido community today.

In fact, while the authors do not subscribe to the unusual - and often quasi-religious practices of many modern clubs, they do respect the wishes of those individuals to train as they wish.

However, a warning to those about to read this book may be necessary.

In recent years there's been a tendency to ascribe certain existential qualities to the practice and study of Aikido. The authors do not share in these beliefs or practices, and view with distaste the increasingly outlandish behavior of allegedly respectable teachers of this martial art which was once fit for kings.

The following warning is derived from the actions of modern day practitioners and contains quotes spoken by some alleged high-grade teachers.

WARNING:

The following terms and phrases you will not find inside: There will be no mention of "meditating under waterfalls," no "twinkling feelings in the dojo," no instances recalled where someone's brain has "blown out of the head and hovered above their body like a cloud of dust; then filtered back while creating lights into the abdomen with a flower opening sensation." In this book we will not talk about harmonizing with the planets," or "being at one with the universe." If you want twinkling, meditation or harmonization, you won't find it here. If you want to learn about traditional technique and its history as well as enjoy some interesting stories about the early days of Aikido, then read on.

If you want to improve your abilities as a martial artist, then put this book down and train hard. On the mat is where it's at.

With that said, it should be explained that the martial arts as a whole are like an ocean and everyone has a cupful of the water. Some are claiming that their cupfuls are the entire ocean, and others are claiming that their cupfuls are bigger, better or stronger. But really it is the sum-total of all of these cups which makes the ocean of technique interesting and complete. It's important to understand that a school of technique shouldn't be compared to the water in the cup - but rather to the cup itself. The water of technique is always changing - adapting to whatever tries to contain it.

From the early group of British Aikido pioneers in the 1950s, the handful that still practice and teach are:
• Sensei Ken Williams who is the head of the "Ki Federation of Great Britain."
• Mr. Hayden Foster who is the principal coach of the "Institute of Aikido" and a long-time friend of both Henry Ellis and Derek Eastman. Ellis met with Foster in the 1950s at the Hut. He trained with him on the first day he started Aikido and they have been friends ever since, always keeping in contact.

• Mr. Ralph Reynolds is the principal of the "Aikido Fellowship of Great Britain." Mr. Reynolds also keeps in regular contact with Foster, Ellis and Eastman.

Aikido makes many grand statements about "Aiki," love and harmony, yet there is more bitterness and enmity in the Aikido community than any of the other martial arts, so the hard traditional training and values that Kenshiro Abbe Sensei hammered into these original pioneers is perhaps even more vital today than it was then.

After almost 50 years, these men are all still great friends - a clear indication that those early values work.

Positive Aikido

This book contains nearly all the learning and experience gathered in a single school and its developing organization over the past 48 years. The authors have worked hard to leave nothing out - although there will no doubt be gaps , items we wish we'd included, and information which other schools would contest or dispute. We have tried, however to provide the reader with a complete package. This book does not contain the history of Aikido. It is not aimed at providing the complete philosophy of Aikido. And it does not pretend to encompass all of what Aikido currently is and is becoming. This is a book about one school's philosophy, history, technique, and continuing concerns.

The contents of this book includes:

Forward

SPIRIT

Positive attitude - the foundation for Aikido
An exploration of the necessary focus for positive action. This section describes the physical and mental aspects of the individual in combat.

MIND

Integrity
A section on morality in the martial arts. Here the authors have provided articles aimed at both the student and the teachers of modern Aikido and martial arts in general.

BODY

Practicum
All the technique currently being taught in the Ellis Schools to include a section on troubleshooting for students from all organizations, instructions for applying and learning technique, and more than 1000 sequence photos and illustrations detailing each attack and defense. A section on weapons technique is also included.

THE ELEMENTS OF TRADITION

Histories
A look at the birth of British Aikido, the early students and teachers and the fantastic journey Aikido has made from Japan to Britain and on to the United States.

Oral tradition
A grouping of stories from the early days of Aikido in Britain - some insightful, and some just unusual or humorous. Often, its with these stories that real lessons are learned.

Teachers
This is a section containing the biographies of the teachers who have influenced our school's technique. Among them are some of the most senior Aikido teachers of modern times.

The Positive Approach

The following section attempts to describe the necessary attitude to enter into combat. It is an exploration of the foundation of good martial art skills and practices as employed by members of our school..

The contents of this section includes:

The place where things happen
The Positive
Stance
Attitude
Extension
Intention
Movement
Focus
Relaxation
Breathing
Change
Timing
Discipline
Simplicity
Hard-Practice
Determination

A Summary

The place where things happen

There is a line.

At one end of the line stand those who would say combat is all about what is effective. What is not effective has no worth. At the other end of the line stand those who say that the pursuit and development of spirit is the most important task - because with proper spirit, the fight becomes less of a contest of strength; and more of a puzzle of cooperation.

The line has a center.

At that center - as with all centers - there is a twisting mass of conflict. Are we animal or are we spiritual? Are we instinctual or are we intellectual? Is there meaning in life, or is life the meaning?

The center of that line is the blade's edge. This is the place which is neither hard nor soft - but both.

If you look at the things which matter in life - the things which shape us and guide us from one experience to another - it's possible to see that the important things are occuring on this edge. They are products of the conflict perpetually occuring from the meeting of these two opposing forces. This is the place where balance is either maintained or lost - a place between what is safe and what is not, between what is hard and what is soft, between what is animal and what is spiritual. This is the place where life-changing decisions are made, and where the effects of these decisions have the most meaning.

Technique is no different from life; and the mat is just a microcosm of the world which exists outside of it. Those who say that a thing must be only effective are as wrong as those who say a thing must be focused on spirituality before anything else.

Technique and life are more than being effective, and they are more than being focused on the spirit - they are more, because they are less of both of these.

To make the changes necessary in life and on the mat, we have to find and constantly maintain the balance on the edge of whatever is the center - that is where things are dynamic, and that is where it is possible to maintain positive attitude and motion.

The positive

Positive attitude and motion is achieved prior to the application of technique. It is at the same time, the foundation of all good technique - and the result of practicing good technique.

In the beginning of training, a student will try to force his body to accomplish the necessary movement. In this early stage, attention is focused on the broad aspects of large movement - where should the hands be? Where should the feet be? Where should the hips be? These questions are answered in this beginning time. Little thought is given - or should be given - to other matters. Broad-based motion is the foundation material. Diluting it with other concerns is pointless and dangerous.

As the student progresses, the elements of this broad-based motion will be learned and finer adjustments will be made until the movement is technically correct. Still, no other matters should be considered.

Once the technical aspects are conquered, the student faces further refinements in the motion. This may include finer, more fluent motion in which the various steps inside each technique are blended to make something more effective and complete.

Still, no thought should be given to anything other than the refinement of the physical technique.

As the student becomes more energetic in the performance of technique, and the movement becomes more fluid, attention should be paid toward the physical aspect achieved before and after the technique. Does the practitioner appear to be confident? Do they appear to be on balance and ready to move again? Are they projecting something from within their stance and attitude?

Stance

Stance is one of the first things learned in many martial arts - yet it so often enters the training regimen without proper description.

In Aikido, the stance is relaxed - but not purposeless. By keeping our lead hand and trailing hand low, we offer our opponent a target to attack. By keeping our feet closer together, with slight bend in our knees, we make our profile smaller, allowing forward and backward movement to be fast, without using too much energy.

These principles are not new to the world - they are practiced every day by students of strategy, businessmen and regular people.

For example, a person working retail notices that at the end of the day, there is money missing from the till. So, they leave the keys for the till out where they can be watched. In this way, they can see who is taking money from the register. So, they assumed a stance of vulnerability in order to more effectively strike their opponent.

The classic movie, The Seven Samurai, illustrates this point as well. The protectors of the village in the film build strong defenses everywhere but in one location, so that the villans will be funneled down the killing space they have created.

Those who build a strong stance have to defend strongly according to their opponent's decisions. Those who build a "smart" stance have only to move at their liesure - they have already made the decisions for their opponent.

In a similar way, the profile you create for yourself in an environment can subsequently determine speed and maneuverability. The more you sacrifice speed and maneuverability - the more you have to compensate with strength, power and size.

In Aikido, the stance brings the feet relatively close together with good spring in the knees and hips turned squarely toward the opponent. Contact with the ground is total and the body's weight is centered.

This profile is substantially smaller than that created by many styles of gung-fu or some of the more traditional schools of Karate. The smaller profile, however, means speed and maneuverability without having to add substantial weight in muscles and improvements in breathing and delivery of force.

This item as well, is used often in today's world.

To use our retail analogy again, we'd have to look at that company versus its competitors - As long as the company is small, it can move on various deals and promotions quickly and efficiently. When too many people clutter up the works, however, the sheer weight of the business, salaries, loss through theft, insurance and benefits, outside costs, increases in the money spent on marketing - can all serve to bury the company.

Successful big businesses exist because they are so huge. They purchase items at lower cost and subsequently can afford huge marketing campaigns. They are often slow and graceless, but their tactics of size and strength allow them to keep on winning.

Attitude

Attitude is the physical position we take when facing a problem. This is where the methods of "Positive" technique can be most clearly seen and understood.

When we face an opponent or a problem, we are either overwhelmed and subsequently fail or we are resolute, taking control and overcoming the opposition. In either case, it is possible to see that good or bad attitude will have an effect on the outcome.

Looking at this from the perspective of a salesman, this issue becomes clear.

In order for his customer to believe in the product and make a purchase, the salesman must believe, or appear to believe in the product himself. The customer, taken in by the salesman's use of language and posture, will soon hand over his money.

In technical application on the mat or in combat, this idea is no different. In order for you to succeed against your opponent, you must first have taken his mind.

Nakazono Sensei - one of the old school, Aikido teachers once told reporters in Britain, "strong mind - strong body." By this he meant if your mind is strong, then whatever is happening with your body can be overcome, and the result will be a "strong body" which succeeds against all odds. By the same token, if your mind is weak, it does not matter how much physical strength you possess. Failure in this case is almost assured.

Positive attitude is a bit of a pardox, because although it creates good technique, it also requires good technique to continue to accomplish it.

As an example, we may decide to climb a hill and engage the enemy, but if we do this poorly, our strong attitude may waver and everything collapses. Or, to bring this in terms of Aikido, we may decide to demonstrate a technique for a class full of students - or for a promotion test. As we step out onto the mat, we are mentally prepared with our positive attitude intact. Yet, as we move into our technique, a mistake is made, our concentration is blown and the positive attitude we began with is forgotten as we attempt to find our balance.

So, attitude is important - and it is more than just a state of mind. When we speak of attitude, we are talking about a combination of factors: stance (or posture), movement, mental focus, and extension.

Extension

Many confuse extension with some kind of mystical power. When it is talked about, it is invariably linked to Ki or Kokyu. Nakazono Sensei once wrote that when the early Dan grades were with O'Sensei Ueshiba, they had asked him about the properties of Ki and Kokyu - Ueshiba chose not to answer, saying that hard practice was the key to understanding these things and that Ki and Kokyu could not be talked about. He further stated that those who did talk about them were liars.

You will therefore hear nothing about Ki and Kokyu from me.

Instead I will tell you about extension, which is a very physical property of technique.

With extension, the body is using positive attitude to move into a position where it can best apply technique - or it is moving out of a position, making a throw or joint lock with good positive attitude.

Here is an indication of how this works: As your opponent attacks, you enter into their space with positive attitude. The opponent is unbalanced by this counter-attack, and struggles to regain his position of strength. There is, however, not enough time for this to happen and your opponent is placed into a position which he can not easily escape from. The conclusion of the technique uses the same outward pressure introduced in your entry. The application of this force is extension.

I will echo a previous sentiment.

This concept is best understood through hard practice.

In addition, I'd like to point out that by utilizing methods currently in practice in many modern schools of Aikido - extension cannot be understood or practiced properly. This is a martial concept which can be applied to strategy in many forms. It is a concept and practice used by commanders in battle, and subsequently does not translate well to an environment where practitioners are dancing around each other like fairies, talking about the planets, the universe and the lovely bean sprouts they are growing in their garden this year.

In order to effectively practice extension, you must be able to enter strongly. This requires that your practice partner be strong enough to absorb such an entry, and also requires that your partner is attacking with intention.

Intention

Most American High Schools host dances for their students at various times during the year. Many young people will likewise be intimately familiar with the currents of popularity and peer pressure associated with their day-to-day lives in the Junior High and High School environment.

These currents are fueled by youthful lack of experience in the matters of life, bodies surging with hormones, and the need for acceptance - or to understand the what and why of things.

All these opposing forces are in place as these kids go to their first dance.

For the first hour or two, the boys are on one side of the gymnasium and the girls on the other - two nervous circles of people, until someone crosses that gap, chooses a partner and "breaks the ice."

As that initial choice is made and the first dancer starts out to find his partner - that is intent.

We can see this on the mat within our own technique.

As the opponent makes ready for his attack, many Aikido students today will wait for their opponent to come, then take a technique which almost requires the opponent to fall down for them. This ridiculous display has no more martial application than the dancing happening in those high school gyms.

Instead, when facing an opponent, the practioner of strong Aikido technique will face with intention. That is to say, they will face their opponent with the dual knowledge that they are going to not only survive the encounter, but also take their opponent totally.

The attacker is aware of this fact before he moves because everything about his opponent is speaking of strength. This is intention.

The samurai had an idea which many believed in - that it was "better to rush in." This meant that while it is possible that failure could result from moving in with intent, at least they would fail having done something.

The development of intention can be linked to extension because without intent, extension is impossible.

Intention, however, cannot be practiced - it can only be developed and nurtured. It is not a physical thing like the principle of extension. Purely an internal concept, intention is all about "Siezing the Day" - or perhaps it could be better put into words as "siezing the moment."

To do this, however, you must be able to really move.

Movement

Movement is often talked about in conjuction with lofty ideas and terminology. It is, however, nothing more than attack and defense.

As our opponent is attacking, so are we. Our defense in Aikido lies in the fact that we are moving along the same line in which the attack is coming. In application this is either an issue of moving directly into our opponent with irimi, or moving into our opponent in a more oblique fashion - tai sabaki.

When we consider movement, it's useful to take it off the mat for a moment.

Consider two competing businesses. Each is in a small-town market and each sees an opportunity to expand into a nearby community. One of these does all the appropriate studies, makes all the proper inquiries, investigates the locale they want to move to and begins to look at real-estate.

The other businessman knows that he is in competition and whoever makes a positive step into the new area first, will have the advantage. So he forgoes the usual red-tape and moves directly into a facility in the new town. He spends his time instead on rennovation, advertising and name recognition amongst the new population. He is in-place a year before his competition arrives and is well established.

The second businessman did not worry about the mechanics of movement - he simply moved.

In the same way, Aikido - or any martial art - technique is properly executed. To concern yourself with the mechanics of the thing will only serve to make static what should be fluid. Combat is about movement. Nothing is static in this environment.

In fact, it could be said that through movement, we influence or control our environment.

Controlling the environment

Modern Aikido practitioners want to talk about cooperation and being in harmony with the attacker and the environment.

I have a theory about harmony: If the opponent attacks, and I return the attack at the same moment, taking him with control and power; that is harmony. He doesn't have to cooperate with me, and he doesn't have to work with me. He can try his best to kill me and I'll take him down with devastating effect. That is control - and that is harmony - the harmony of all things in nature- the opponent moves in, we enter stongly and take him totally.

When we enter a space where there is potential for conflict, many will either freeze to the spot or over-react. Our opponent, or opponents are also mortal and will behave in accordance with the rules which guide all of us. While we may be struck with hesitation or fear - so will they.

Subsequently, it's important to enter this space with controlled power, intent and positive attitude. By doing this, you will exert immediate control over your surroundings. From this higher ground, you can sweep into your opponents, destroying each one in turn. Remaining outside of their circle, you can contain them and redirect them into each other.

You can use their bodies and the situation as a means to control the environment as a whole.

In effect, this goes back to "strong mind-strong body," because if you can take the minds of those opposing you, you in effect have controlled them. Their weak minds led to slow or half-hearted responses and ultimately led to their undoing.

The military has been aware of this notion ever since there has been a military force on the planet. From the terrifying masks and armor of the Japanese Samurai to the leaflet drops in Iraq and the blaring American music at Checkpoint 77 in Mogadishu, Somalia, Psychological Operations have been waged against various "enemies" throughout time.

The very first early human who picked up a very large club and brandished it at a fellow individual, was using this same idea. This has little to do with harmony in the current sense of that word - It has everything to do with perceived threat and strength.

To make any of this happen, however, requires focus.

Focus

When a technique is taken, or a movement is entered into, concentration on that moment when you first engage the opponent must be total. To let this "focus" waver could mean disaster.

This of course holds true for many situations inside and outside the world of martial arts.

And odly enough, it brings us back to the beginning of this writing. Because at the point where we lose focus, we begin to get lost amidst various fantasies and beliefs not based on fact or the simple, practical execution of good, solid technique.

As an example, my teachers recently attended a seminar in Britain in which several fellow Aikido teachers participated and demonstrated technique.

One of these spent ages blathering-on about angles and direction whilst placing various large, red velcro-backed arrows on the mat. At the end of this discussion, the mat resembled a weather map, but it seemed that little was gained from the lecture. Where did this guy lose his focus?

In another instance which I witnessed myself, an alleged Dan grade trotted out onto the mat at the Crystal Palace in London, two assistants following dutifully behind him. As I looked on astonished, this guy layed down on the mat and the two assistants picked him up by his neck and ankles and turned him around, then set him back on the mat. This kokyu exercise - really a simple trick - was supposed to be his demonstration of Aikido technique. Where did he lose his focus?

Need more? What about the times you're practicing with a character who assures you that the reason a technique doesn't work is because they aren't at their best - their "ki" is going north or south - or the damned stars aren't lined up right. Are these reasons or excuses? I've seen alleged high grade teachers try to tell me that one thing or another thing will work if it is done "for real," but refuse to prove this point. I would rather take a bad fall, break a limb or otherwise get injured on a good technique, than witness garbage like this. What is the root cause?

All these things are questions of focus. As soon as we lose our place in the world - or as soon as we lose our place in a fight, we are lost. Focus is an absolute must to remain effective in any part of our lives.

The way to maintain focus in a fight is to continually assess your goals. Have you dealt with the matter properly at each given moment? Does the situation require that you elevate the intensity of your response? Do you need to relax more?

The maintenance of focus outside of martial concerns remains the same, however. In these instances, an individual should be taking stock of their environment and the way they are using it. By staying objective, you can remain in-focus and effective. In order to accomplish this objectivity, however, you must remain relaxed.

Relaxation

When the opponent attacks, we are met with an age-old dillema - attack or retreat. Most will back-off to try to come to grips with a stuation which is developing too rapidly for them to follow. Some will freeze in place as the opponent hits them - and a few will enter with the same vigor as their opponent.

In this moment, as the fight is begun, the tendency in each of these cases is to fall victim to some time of emotional response - be it fear, horror or surprise.

This is a mistake. The entry into a fight should be a thing devoid of emotion. Dealing with the attack as if it were a business transaction (your opponent comes to you for a service - you provide it - he pays for it) is the safest way to avoid undue tenseness in the limbs. If you enter a technique with too much adrenaline on board, you'll use too much energy, and the defense will fail. If you do not remain centered in your emotions and relaxed in your responses, you'll have little flexibility to change direction in your defense.

Relaxation is key for all types of problems on and off the mat.

As an example, the Japanese katana is a very thin, extremely sharp instrument. When examined, it appears as any knife or sword - to be made out of a single slab of metal. In fact, the design of this weapon has been refined over more than 800 years. An original blade is comprised of no less than two hardnesses of metal. The result is a blade which has the ability to "relax" as it cuts through the target.

This flex should be also applied to the warrior. Relaxation is the key to clear thought, clarity is the key to focus. Often, relaxation is tied directly to breathing and breath control.

Breathing

Today, one of the things obsessed about in modern schools of Aikido is breathing.

Rightly so.

Breath control is the key to bringing all the other factors into cooperation with each other. Breath could be seen to be the glue which holds our technique together and adds the final polishing-step necessary to make what we do effective.

Breathing is the tide of our human existance - like the ocean, there is a low and a high tide. As we breath in we are weak. When we breath out, we are strong. In this respect, engaging an opponent on the mat is no different than engaging him on the battlefield. With breath timed appropriately to the technique, we generate tremendous force and strength and can easily overwhelm our opponent.

All technique in Aikido is properly executed in this way: breathing in as you accept the opponent's attack, and breathing out as you engage and defeat him.

As we relax and breath in the fight, less energy is expended and the technique is more effective against our opponent.

Breath is not expended with resignation, however. Breathing is accomplished with a sense of gladness that the fight is once again joined.

It's perhaps important to understand this point above all others.

Many modern-day Aikido practitioners - and even some of the old-school teachers who have moved on to other studies, have involved themselves in the belief that a world of lasting peace is possible. The human condition, however tells us other things. Still, many of these peace-oriented folks will point to the fact that it is possible, if everyone works together, that lasting peace can be attained. Ueshiba himself said that peace could be achieved through Budo.

Perhaps he was talking about personal peace - if so, that seems logical.

For those who would like to believe that total world peace would be a wonderful thing, I would ask "at what cost?"

Human kind has a pretty poor track record in this area. The odds are better that we will continue to fight amongst ourselves, let children starve all over the world, pollute our planet, etc.

But is discord, disagreement and fighting such a bad thing.

These negative things are constantly met by the positive - and it's on this testing ground that new ideas are forged, new frontiers crossed and new life created. This is why I say that when we breathe in we are entering the fight with happiness - because by doing so we've placed ourselves once again on that blade-edge center; with victory or failure riding on our shoulders, but also with the certainty that something is going to happen. This is the place where we can make a difference and where change is constant.

Change

When we talk about change in martial art, we can be saying many different things. There's constant movement in the fight which always requires a fluid change of direction, technique posture and balance to make things happen; there's change in the way we see ourselves and our art as we age and gain more experience, and there's change in the way techniques must be applied as new skills or limitations are gained.

Many modern Aikido students would point out that "change" is the reason the current-day technique is superior to the old. I have had people tell me that the technique has been refined to be more effective.

O'Sensei Ueshiba may have been concerned deeply with religion - but most who studied under him have said that he was a brilliant practitioner of the fighting arts. In fact, Kenshiro Abbe told my teacher about the first time he met Ueshiba. That experience is recounted at the beginning of this book. If Ueshiba was capable of taking out someone as physically strong and technically adept as Abbe - he certainly must have had some fantastic abilities.

How then could so many people in so many modern clubs believe that they are smarter than O'Sensei - smart enough to alter his original technique and make something that is "more effective." In fact, I have found just the opposite in most of my admittedly limited travels. I have found dojos where the practice is a good aerobic workout, but where there is no strength in the limbs of the practitioners - no concept of the reality of an attack.

My teachers have experienced this slow decline in positive technique over the last 30 years. Their frustration and disgust were partly what fueled this book.

So, when we talk about change in this respect, it is a change which should not be occuring. In too many cases, Aikido is not evolving - it is devolving. The changes wrought on the original technique are nothing but fantasy supported by assumption - that is to say, nothing is tested in reality. However, it's important to note here that there are a great many people who are not interested in reality.

Added to this acid-bath are the dojos which are practicing the technique of O'Sensei when he was an old man. Many of the original Dan grades who trained with Ueshiba were heard to say in the 1960s that they did not fully comprehend where Ueshiba's strength was coming from - that he was extremely powerful and they had been given to understand that this power was more "spiritual" than anything else.

I would not dispute the words of these great teachers who were there and experienced these things.

However, Ueshiba's abilities followed a lifetime of powerful technique. So it seems odd to me that so many people want to emulate the older O'Sensei rather than the younger one. It is as if they want to skip the early lessons and move directly to master level. Perhaps this is a part of the modern 20th century fast-food mentalitiy. People do not want to hear that the path to understanding and enlightenment is blocked with obstacles called pain and frustration. They want "change" now.

In the early forms of the Aikido techniques, change was all about continued application. In other words, the technique was taken until it began to fail, then it was changed to another - in the end, a myriad of movements conspired to take the opponent. The ability to do this is achieved through continued hard practice in which the attacks are strong and made with intent. This does not mean that techniques need to be interchanged half-a-dozen times to take the opponent. If the entry is positive, and the technique applied correctly, there will be no need for further movement. - when Aikido is done properly, there's no need for a bunch of wide, circular movement or technique - you only need one.

Timing

To make change in your technique, however, requires good timing.

Timing is in everything we do. If you look at the places in your life where things have had an almost magical quality to them - you can probably see that there was good timing involved somewhere.

On the mat, this is the same. As technique is applied, it is timing which allows us to safely enter and unbalance our opponent.

Take for example, Tenchinage. This is a movement deeply involved with proper timing. If we look at an attack with yokomen (side of head cut), it's necessary to meet the cut before it ever enters your space. In fact, your timing should be such that you are moving as your opponent begins his motion. This will allow you to properly intercept the attacking limb before it even leaves your opponent's space.

Our timing is tied to our breathing - breath in as we move in; breath out as we take our opponent. This is timed perfectly with our opponent's speed and movement. The result of this is what many new-age dojos would call "blending."

In fact, it has little to do with matching your opponent's movement or intention - and more to do with matching their timing. We are not dancing with our opponent - we are taking him with a martial technique. Subsequently the word "blending" is probably poorly chosen. "Taking," really says it all. We are assuming control of our opponent and our environment by using the many priciple's being outlined for you in this book. Each principle is applied to the fight carefully and with good timing. This is why the resulting motion appears smooth and powerful.

For this kind of thing to work, though, means that you must only move at the appropriate times. To make entry at the wrong moment - or to apply a portion of a technique out of sequence with your opponent will cause some very serious problems. So, you must remain disciplined.

Discipline

This is an area which is adhered to by most Aikido schools throughout the world in various ways.

We should pay attention to the fact that this word can have many different meanings in the application of our chosen arts. In fact, discipline could be taken to mean "the strength to continue to pass on our art form as it was intentended."

An example of this not occuring in today's world is the simple press-up exercise which has been abandoned by most modern Aikido clubs. This exercise - in which press-ups (or push-ups) are accomplished with the backs of the wrists in contact with the mat instead of the palms of the hands, is a very old exercise probably dating back hundreds of years.

It not only increases the strength in the joints of the wrists, elbows and shoulders, but also builds muscle at the appropriate points to aid in the accomplishment of technique. It is a painful, unpleasant exercise which never ceases to be difficult.

Few Aikido clubs currently practice this. Some even say now, that this is bad for your wrists. Yet I have done these exercises for 15- 20 years now. My teachers have done them for 45 years. Their teachers before them, performed these things as well. In ten years of teaching, I have not had one student who didn't benefit from these exercises - in fact, one student who had lost the feeling in his left hand as a child when a nerve was severed, regained feeling in that hand after just a few months of hard practice.

So why is this exercise no longer practiced by most schools? Two possible reasons - because it's painful and few care to do it anymore, or because somewhere along the line, the curriculum was changed and the exercise was lost.

Understand you don't have to agree with me, but I believe in both of these cases, a lack of discipline can be found.

Discipline extends into other areas of our lives as martial artists and as regular people.

Some of the stories or lessons you will find in this book to be unusual or outrageous. But these remembrances speak in ways we can easily understand, about many attributes of good and bad martial artists - an effective and not-so-effective people.

Discipline can also be applied to the minute details of our technique - do we run our customary mile before class today? Or do we cop-out? Do we push ourselves to do one more sit-up, one more push-up - one more ukeme, one more technique than we did before? Or do we have an easy day of it, go home and drink some beer? In this way, the job of becoming strong people is never finished. We are constantly creating ourselves every moment of every day. The choices we make on and off the mat can lead to a positive mentality - or a more negative one depending on our ability to remain mentally disciplined

Staying positive will ensure stronger, more effective technique and will allow us to continue to keep our methods and approaches to everything in life direct and simple.

Simplicity

Our ability to maintain a balance amidst all these varied aspects I have described could seem to be overwhelming if we were attempting to apply each and every one through a merely intellectual means.

Most of us can concentrate on more than one thing at a time - but few could keep tabs of all these complex aspects at one time. How then do we incorporate these tools to ensure the proper development of our students? And how can we as students expect to develop into strong, positive people unless we can ensure each of these various areas are satisfied?

I believe the answer is in simplicity.

In fact, the mistake many new-age students are making is in making their art more complicated than it is. They choose to analyze and break down every small aspect of what they do - allegedly to make them more precise and effective.

Analysis requires perspective. To gain perspective you must have training and experience.

I think the problem many of these young men and women are having stems from a tendency to get their questions answered too early - and not completely when they do.

When I was first learning Aikido in Britain in the 1980s, I had a healthy amount of terror every class. My teachers were imposing, powerful and dangerous characters and when they did take technique on me it was always an extremely painful and physically draining experience. When a question was asked, it was answered by having technique applied. You soon learned to figure out what you could through your own means and leave the rest for another day.

Looking back on this, I think I had the best training possible. Because my teachers stressed technique, performance and effectiveness before anything else, I was brought up in Aikido with a positive mental attitude, strong technique, a deep respect for others, and a healthy disdain for complex explanations or the intellectual and spiritual ramblings of many current-day teachers.

Understand this: I do not call into question the use of concentrating on the more esoteric aspects of Aikido - I call into question the usefulness of investigating these things too early in one's training, or in placing these investigations and studies before everything else in the practice of a martial art.

This ties back into what I said early on: There is a balance which must be struck between these intellectual / spritual aspects and the physical / effectiveness aspects.Concentrating on any one side for too long destroys this balance and sends you down that merry garden path.

When you are new to a martial art, however, you don't know the difference between these two sides of the street. This is where it is important to have a good, well-educated and well-grounded teacher. If you want to be sure you're maintaining a balance, however, there's only one thing you need to do - practice hard on the mat. Everything you need to know and learn is there and will come to you in time.

Hard practice

When we talk about hard practice, some people don't understand.

Hard practice does not mean that we are smashing each other neadlessly about the mat. By working hard, we mean we are as attackers, coming in strong and on balance - not giving ourselves away to our opponent, but rather, providing the appropriate amount of resistance and force according to their grade. If they are a senior kyu grade and you are a junior, you should be attacking them strongly, and they should be taking you as gently as possible. If you are equal in grade, you should be training as equals - attacking as hard and defending as hard as your opponent is. If you are attacking a Dan grade, you should be going in with everything you've got.

This is the best way to train. It develops strong, confident and capable people, and it develops effectiveness all on its own.

Cooperation should exist to some extent when you are learning the technique, however, because without working together, you cannot improve.

When you look at the ways techniques are applied in many modern dojos, you'll see uke "falling down" for his opponent. First, he'll trot in like some dog on a leash, then grasp his opponent halfheartedly and finally fall down - sometimes before his opponent has actually applied the technique. This kind of behavior is ridiculous, and it only serves to blacken the reputation of what once was a beautiful and effective martial art.

Some would call the hard-practicing Aikido club Aikijutsu - I would say, however, that the trotting and falling that is being passed for Aikido in some of the modern schools, could be no more considered Aikido than synchronized swimming.

Was that too harsh?

Look around, visit a couple clubs - this isn't a situation restricted to Aikido - I only use Aiki as an example because that is where my experience lies. However, I have many friends who have had absolutely unbelievable experiences in visiting some dojos, dojangs and kwoons.

When we talk about core values, "hard practice" has to be one of the most important ideas. However, before this aspect is put into motion, there's got to be a foundation of history, proper technique and safety. All these things are learned at a good school. If you want to learn how to find a school appropriate to you, reference the ethics section of this book.

Once the foundation is layed however, and a school is beginning to work toward good hard practices, it is necessary to understand that hard practice only comes with determination.

Determination

This is a quality which can be infused into a person, but which often comes from a combination of life-experiences working in concert with a solid goal.

For example, there has been a young man in my club who started with us when he was 14-years-old. He was considered a troublemaker in school when he was younger, and exercised control in his life by smashing the hell out of people. When he was brought to us, he was a person who had seen little encouragement and a lot of the rougher aspects of life. From our first meeting, however, I knew he was something special, because even though his every attack ended with him lying on the ground, he never quit trying.

Our first "practice" consisted of nothing but continued attacks - and yet he never stopped.

It was this kind of determination and strength the Samurai were said to appreciate a great deal. The Carp is used as a symbol ofr these ancient warriors and appears on artwork with Samurai because of its great strength.

How did our young man come by his determination? I believe it was through focused training in the classroom of life. Why does he still have and use this strength? I believe this is because he has a goal.

He wants to join the U.S. Marines.

Each of us can demonstrate this ability at times by going one more mile; or by taking our day to day problems one step further to find the solution. It is this quality more than anything else, which allows us to progress as people - or as martial artists. Without determination, there can be no "hard practice," but there can also be no discipline, no focus, timing, control of the environment - or many of the other principles I have outlined here. Determination is the mother of many things in the complete warrior.

A summary

An understanding

What we see as reality is often viewed through the colored glass of experience and knowledge. These two things can bind us and blind us as sure as a roll of duct tape. Although we tell ourselves we are on the correct path, our own basis for decisions cants our viewpoint. The result can be dangerous. One of my teachers, Sensei Derek Eastman mentioned a time when he entered a boxing ring as a young man. He thought himself unstoppable at the time, but despite this view, barely remembers leaving the ring.

I have myself visited and practiced with many clubs and have friends in many disciplines. I entered the shootfighting ring once and although I had a good time, found myself bested by an opponent who probably was within my abilities to control. I am aware that I have limitations - either imposed upon me or created by me.

I am also in acceptance of this fact and attempt to work around it and with it.

Still, we have to understand that time and experience must eventually begin to overtake us, and as such our habits in training may subsequently be altered.

The environment - always in conflict - is always in a state of change. How can we expect that we ourselves, our lives, our art should be any different.

At its best, Aikido is said to aim toward harmony - yet the world itself is in constant conflict and change. To try to even understand our place in this seems to rest in the hands of priests.

When I began this book, it started as a guide for the students of my class. In that time, I had learned technique and believed that each movement was complex and specific. Now I believe what I believed before I ever set foot in a martial art class -movement is just movement. and change just is.

14

Sensei Henry Ellis and his assistant, Anita Wilson.

Above: Sensei Ellis and his son, Richard in 1992.

Left: The first U.S. Aikido branch of the Ellis Schools in 1991. Included in this picture are such memorable characters as Tom Macon, Aida Prazak, Ed Madsen, Abbe Brown and Dr. Doug Patrick.

Left: Tada Sensei takes ikkyo on Sensei Ellis at the Bracknell Sports Center during the National Summer School Course, 1969.

Left: The information board which hung for many years on the wall of The Hut. Kyu Shin Do, was a martial art designed by Kenshiro Abbe Sensei.

Below: Sensei Henry Ellis takes shihonage on Sensei David Warne in the 1970s at the Basingstoke Sports Center.

Ethics

The following section contains articles on several distinct aspects of ethics and morality in Aikido and the martial arts in general. That a section such as this one should need to be added to a book on this subject suggests the sad state of decline these arts have descended into. I believe the factors described in this section to be the very areas which must undergo change if the combat arts are to survive in a recognizable and effective form in the future.

The contents of this section includes:

The three aspects of a warrior are mind, body and spirit. Without these three items in place, joining combat means likely destruction at the hands of the opponent. Mind body and spirit can also be referred to by their associated shapes: The circle, square and triangle. Like a circle or sphere, the mind should remain open on all sides, capable of easy expansion, flexible and strong when attacked and able to repel, envelop or move around the attack. The square in combat represents the body which is solid on all sides. The strong body stands firmly in place like a heavy box; difficult to move but with weight and potential motion waiting inside of it. The triangle is the spirit of the warrior in that it has the weight and potential of the box focused to a fine and dangerous point. Spirit or intention sustains the mind and body in the fight.

Forward

Where are we as martial artists going?

I'm not sure.

What I do know is that technique is getting sloppier, public opinion is at an all-time low, and supposition is taking the place of "use it once you know it works."

I see people taking money for questionable services – I see tiny children being given Black Belts for learning a series of Dance routines.

In short, there's a lot of decay in the Martial Arts – physically, effectively and morally. It's a terrible question mark for those just beginning to understand their place within the martial art community.

And I don't know if there's an answer.

Beginnings are always painful.

But it's important to remember that pain is there to remind you that you're still alive.

If you're considering a beginning in the study of the martial arts, or you have decided to train for professional fighting, there's an important aspect of this you should be aware of from the start. When you decide to add a skill to your list of personal abilities, it always takes on a life of its own.

What do I mean? Well, look at a carpenter as an example.

My cousin is married to a carpenter. When they were looking at buying a house, this man decided he could do it himself. Now, he may never have thought when he was younger that he would someday build a house almost single-handedly, but that's what he did. The skill he'd dedicated his life to had eventually caused him to spend months building that house.

In the same way, a choice to pursue a combat skill is more than just that single decision. The study of any combat skill means that eventually it may need to be put to use. And that use can have a devastating meaning for someone else.

So the first thing I suggest to new students is that they seriously consider what they're getting themselves into. If they study at a good club, their technique will become a Danger to everyone around them. They must always keep good discipline and be sure to use what they've learned appropriately. If they are practicing at a good club this self-discipline will come as part of what they are learning.

This is not, however, something to obsess about. Training well and hard is the first and most important consideration in the beginning.

But how do you get there? Let's look at how to choose a martial art and a good martial art club.

In my experience, there are four basic categories of martial art instruction:

• Reality Fighting (no-rules, no-pads, no-kidding)
• Traditional Martial Art study (Historical technique, kata, etiquette, etc.)
• Nontraditional Martial Art study (Altered technique, kata, etiquette, etc.)
• Sport-oriented instruction (Competitors not interested in getting hurt)

We will not say here which of these is better than the other. That is a personal decision. I have experienced each of these in my time as a student and teacher, and I know that I fit in best as a teacher and student of Traditional Art study. However, I do have a number of friends who fit well in those other categories. They are good people, they do not color what they do by saying it is something it is not. They do what they do and they are proud of it.

So, the second thing I urge new students to do is to find that place where they fit the best and not malign those who choose a different path.

The study of the combat arts is perhaps best equated to the purchase of shoes.

If the shoe fits...

To make an informed choice between these four directions, ask yourself why you are getting involved in this stuff.

Looking for Reality Fighting

If you're looking for fighting skills – the ability to handle yourself in a real fight – the best thing to do is to REALLY FIGHT. Honor and rules no longer exist in combat, so to practice as if it does is pointless. If this is the kind of thing you're interested in, get involved in reality fighting – it's often called shoot fighting. If you can't find that kind of thing, look for a wrestling teacher. Most fights end up on the ground anyway. So that's a good place to start. In pursuit of these goals it is important to never be static. Absorb as many skills as possible and make them your own.

Looking for Traditional training

If you're looking for traditional study, there are thousands of clubs out there that will offer this. You have many decisions ahead of you in this case. Almost every country in the world has its own version of stylized combat, so what you face is a veritable buffet of goodies.

Your choice is of course dictated by time, distance and money.

Where are your local training centers? How much to they cost? How long will it take to achieve the goal you have in your mind?

If you find a place which seems to fit within these boundaries, there are additional tests you should put it to. These tests can also be used when you visit schools in the other categories.

• Interview the instructor. Set up an appointment and ask him some pointed questions like:

1. How long has your school been in operation?
2. How many students do you have?
3. How many assistant instructors?
4. Do you have any special programs which can help me achieve my goals?
5. Are there other costs aside from the tuition dues?
6. Do you stress competition?
7. Do you have any references?
8. Do you have any success stories?
9. What are your personal qualifications?
10. Why should I give you my hard-earned money?
11. Do you support any causes?
12. Do you do any community service?
13. What's more important to you; money or helping people?
14. If I had no money to give you, would you still train me?

15. Has anyone ever got injured doing this?

In the assessment of the answers you get back, I will offer you no advice. You must decide yourself if this is the type of person you want teaching you or your children. I will say that the answers to these questions should fall within the following boundaries:

1. A long time.
2. Enough.
3. Enough to assist in the training.
4. Train hard, you'll achieve your goals.
5. No.
6. I stress hard training and personal development.
7. Call the police department, the National Guard, rape crisis groups, the District Attorney's office, other martial art groups; they all know of our club.
8. Many. Let me tell you about some...
9. Look on the walls. My certificates are there.
10. I will do my best to help you achieve the desired end.
11. Some. They are...
12. Our club is involved in...
13. Helping people.
14. Yes.
15. Of course.

• Look at the students in your potential new training hall. How do they act? Do they seem like the kind of person you'd like to be? Would you feel comfortable practicing with them.

• Does the school scare you a little. If the answer is yes, that's good!

Looking for nontraditional training

Unfortunately, in my opinion, many traditional schools have made the mistake of altering their technique permanently.

I will occasionally teach altered technique in my club, but I always tell the students that what they are about to do is something I've developed myself and it may not work for them. I also caution them to remember that the practice of the traditional techniques is what they are graded on and what they should pass on to their students, should they become teachers. The introduction of altered technique is meant as a pleasant distraction.

Still, there are many schools of martial art which teach technique which has been adjusted from the original. In fact, there are whole systems where this has occurred over the course of the last 50 years. Often, the intention of this alteration is to make the system useful in a new environment. As an example, there is an entire grouping of technique in Traditional Aikido that involves sword retention while still cutting your opponent. Although swords are not used by police departments, guns are; and the techniques of this kata can be applied to gun retention.

Sometimes, however, the altered technique takes the place of the original. There are people who believe that this is what happened to Karate. They will point to the traditional kata and stances and say that if the techniques included grappling, many of the strikes would be much more lethal.

Who knows. We weren't there. We can't really say.

We can see changes however in today's technique. I have friends in Tae Kwon Do and Kuk Sool Wan who tell me they are constantly being taught new ways to do old techniques. "Refinements" is the word that is used.

Look, if a thing works, why fix it?

I think that question is what is at the heart of nontraditional training. And I believe it is the reason many martial arts are undergoing facelifts. The teachers believe they are fixing something that's broke. The problem that arises hearkens back to a grade school exercise.

Remember the time the teacher gave one student a message and told them to tell the next student and it got passed to the next and the next, etc. What was the message at the other end?

This is what is happening to traditional martial arts. They get less and less traditional as time goes on.

In fact, a friend of mine recently said he believed so many people were trying to fix the stuff that he didn't think it was worth fixing anymore.

"Dave," he said, "We should really just drop it all and go on from here."

It's really remarkable what has happened in some cases.

State and city police officers I've trained have shown me the technique they learned in the academy.

One such officer, a woman, said of a technique she'd been taught in the academy, "I didn't think that would work."

It's really is such a sad state of affairs.

This is what happens sometimes when technique is altered. Remember, if you change something, while it may work for you, that doesn't mean it will work for everyone. Since the original traditional arts were developed for use by armies of people, it's likely those techniques were meant, tried and proven to be fairly universal. So, perhaps they shouldn't be changed.

Something interesting happens when they're not changed, however.

I received my Aikido training in Britain under Henry Ellis, one of the most senior teachers in the United Kingdom.

Ellis Sensei and Derek Eastman Sensei have been practicing for nearly 50 years. Eastman Sensei once told me that in all that time, they had changed very little. They still practiced the techniques the same they had in the early days.

The late Nakazono Sensei, who was one of Ellis' teachers remarked that Sensei Ellis had changed little, when he met him in Santa Fe 40 years after training the early Aikido groups in Britain.

I was there at the Crystal Palace in Britain when several old teachers came up to Sensei to talk to him.

I still remember what one of them said.

"Sensei, it was great to see you in action again," said the man. "You haven't changed a bit."

It's that refusal to change – to become softer, however, which seems to have alienated the group from the modern-day Aikido practitioners. In an attempt to keep intact what they'd been taught by Kenshiro Abbe Sensei, Nakazono Sensei, Chiba Sensei and others,

they've become an island of high-powered, positive, tight technique in a sea of modern technique which ever seeks to become more circular, gentle, and which calls itself traditional.

Now, which is traditional; the veritable ocean of modern stylists, or the island of hard-liners? Who you talk to dictates the answer to that question, so how do you determine the difference?

It's my experience that many alleged traditional martial artists make the mistake of believing their technique is the be all and end all. Some of these guys will have an answer to everything. All you have to remember is that in a real fight, anything goes, and the other guy is going to resist anything you do. Traditional kata seeks to constrain technique. Modern practitioners attempt to categorize and contain attack and response. Combinations are developed as the final word on defense.

As Bruce Lee explained, a fight is fluid. Therefore the response should also be fluid. Some nontraditional schools seek to embrace this theory, and I must say, if your goal is effective defense, I believe that to be wise.

So, if you're looking for nontraditional training, I would suggest a simple rule of thumb:

Somewhere in between the ultra-practical, high-powered extremely traditional technique and the fluid, changing methods of the no-rules fighter, is where you'll feel most comfortable. Remember, because you're practicing a combination of technique not many other people are, you won't be welcome by the traditionalists, and you won't be welcomed by the reality fighters. You'll forever be in-between – another island.

Looking for Sport-Oriented Instruction

Sport-oriented instruction can be found in the reality fighting, traditional and nontraditional arenas. Almost every school instructor will be able to point you in the direction you want to go. However, when looking at a school's rack of trophies, you should realize that many of them are not what they seem.

Often schools belong to a larger organization comprised of as many as 10 or 12 schools. When you see a trophy for "World Championship," it doesn't necessarily mean that the school competed in a championship match against others from all over the world. What it means is that they competed against the people in their organization, who all came in for competition from the organization's 10 schools. Subsequently, titles can be a bit misleading.

Additionally, trophies and awards may be given to a fighter who competed in a tournament with 500 participants. That may sound good until you find out that in his weight class and division there were only two people. All he had to beat was one guy.

I would say that the best way to gauge a school for sport-fighting is to look at the students and the way the teacher pushes them to do better. Is the sparring done with respect for the opponents? Are the students comfortable fighting each other? Are there sincere handshakes and smiles afterward? Does it look like something you'd be proud to do?

Use some common sense.

Believe in Hard Work

What do you believe? Do you believe in magic? If you do, that's fine, but don't mistake the things you see in martial art demonstrations as magic. They are not.

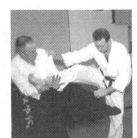

Things shown to you by experienced martial artists are only useful tricks produced through a lot of hard practice.

In more than 20 years I have never seen anything I couldn't attribute to the physical.

If it fascinates you – good. If it causes you to take up training – good. If it suggests to you that you can use some undefined power within you to affect the world around you – you may just have a bad case of gas.

I would never attempt to dissuade the many experienced practitioners of the internal styles who believe that Qi, Ki or Chi is what is behind good martial technique. I could be wrong. However, of this I am not wrong: As a beginning student, you have no business exploring these matters. They will only serve to confuse you and lead you merrily down the garden path.

Ellis Sensei, says it best: "On the mat is where it's at." There's no need to read a bunch of ridiculous books on philosophy, universal oneness and other crap. All you have to do is practice – hard. Realization of these other things will come in time, and you will be able to make your own conclusions.

Sensei Andy Lyon of the Basingstoke club attacks Sensei Ellis with a kick in this photo sequence. The result is painful, but effective.

What did O'Sensei want?

I have seen a tendency in formal Aikido circles to look toward developing technique like the founder of Aikido, Moreihei Ueyshiba.

I have even heard senior teachers say "this is what Ueyshiba intended."

What a bunch of crap!

We don't know what the man intended – nor can we ask him. We can't say why he did particular technique and we can't say why some of it may have worked for him and not for us. But I can offer a good guess.

Ueyshiba spent his life studying martial technique – and using it. He wasn't only a master of the tiny piece of the combat arts pie we call Aikido. He was a practitioner and master of a massive amount of traditional technique. He was the way he was because of his training and experience. To attain the same level of technique, you or I would have to experience the same training and the same life – and still we would probably come out different in the end.

It's useful to know the history of all the arts – and to understand why they were created and what they offered our ancestors. Trying to achieve that same level of technique, however, may be an empty quest.

I will take what I have learned, refine it, teach it and use it to make a difference. I will be mindful of the intentions of my teacher and the teachers which came before him; but I will not follow their path blindly, nor strike out on my own. I will make something good from what I've been given. What will you do?

Losing the Way

We have changed lives. Good martial arts teachers have taken people in need and made important contributions to those lives.

Myself, I've helped a few. I've also lost some along the way – either due to my own stupidity, blindness, or to circumstances I couldn't change.

If you are practicing and for one reason or another, get pulled away from practice – it's not the end. A good martial art teacher is there to help you – and he's not going to hold it against you if you leave for a time. You can always come back – we are always here for you.

> The warrior is unbound. Because the three aspects are balanced within him, he can become anything and change anything. He is like a baby in this respect – probabilities and possibilities flock around him.

A word to the Teacher
What are your intentions?

We need to make a difference.

What more can be said for that quality which is lacking in the lives of us all. How have we made a difference in the lives of others today? How have we affected the world?

As martial artists – indeed, as artists in general; – we should be constantly aware of what our art form is conveying to others. We should take an honest look around and see how we are being viewed by the young people of today.

Why the young people? Because the older fighters and teachers, already set in their ways, will do nothing to endanger the world they've created – be it one of emotional dependence, financial dependence or physical dependence.

What I've found in looking at some of the young men and women is that they're disinterested in the practice of a thing which doesn't work on the street. They do not believe there is any worth in the study of the martial arts. Subsequently, martial art teachers in the West have sought to make the pursuit of these arts "more appealing" to people by lessening or altering the training regimen, shortening the practices, and pushing toward a feel-good, fast-food method of practice.

I'm not saying these techniques are inherently bad – I am saying that they are eroding the very art form so many of us have dedicated such a large part of our lives to study.

This is not just disconnected theory. I have seen this process at work.

In the early 90's I worked in a small Midwest town as a newspaper reporter. During that time, I saw several martial art studios come and go, until one took root. In the beginning, the studio was a small, developing place, with good intentions, solid practice and an instructor who seemed to be sincere in his intention to create a place where his students could practice. After a few years, his studio had expanded to hold almost 200 students. That's when things started to go wrong.

Eventually, he sold his club to a student who went from a third Kyu grade to a 1st Dan overnight.

The club subsequently fell apart, but not before that student had spent every last penny he had, trying to keep it afloat.

Along with the school went the contracts many of the students had signed to exchange exorbitant amounts of money for enrollment in a club which "guaranteed" a black-belt in a certain amount of time.

The end result of this was an empty shop front, disillusioned students and a whole lot of distrust.

It doesn't matter if this was an intentional action - what matters is the result. Unfortunately operating a school is a difficult balance to achieve.

First the complexity of managing such a place seems to require the chief instructor to become just that: a manager. Without his regular practices, he becomes soft, losing touch with the very thing he sought to create – a successful, school which can change people

for the better.

And although this did occur in this instance, there was also another side-effect. The loss of respect for the teacher caused his senior students to question his authority (perhaps rightly so at that point). The resulting discord then caused others to question their pursuit of the art form, and the sum-total of it all was the destruction of the entire school.

This is an outsider's perception of what occurred, however. Just as likely is the following scenario: The higher grade students were entrusted with too much of the operation of the school, and the result was an eroding of the teacher's authority. The resulting discord produced a poor environment for instruction, and the organization collapsed.

Whatever the cause, those who were trained there, in the end had useless pieces of paper for certificates, few real skills, and little discipline. For the children – many of whom were very young at that time – they were given the opportunity to see their parents curse the school and teacher, cast about hopelessly for another place for their child to practice the same martial art, and finally give up in disgust.

This is why I say that the practice of good, traditional combat arts is being eroded.

It is also why I say it's important to look carefully at what we are conveying to others in the pursuit of our art form.

Are we making a difference? Or are we just making it from day-to-day?

Are we in it for the money, or are we in it for the morality?

Are we doing it all for the right reasons?

Don't think you're exempt from this just because the closest you've ever gotten to martial arts is a Jean Claude Van Damme movie. Who are you? What sets you apart from others? What are you good at? How can you make a difference in the lives of others. You don't have to be a professional fighter to fight, and you don't have to be a mechanic to turn a wrench.

Saying you have nothing to offer is just a cop-out.

We've all seen the kids standing on the corner by our schools, shuffling around in the dust, smoking a cigarette with that disinterested, glazed look in their eyes. They got that way because nobody really tried to help them be any different. Nobody stopped to listen when they asked questions. Nobody cared.

You want to know how to save the world? Start with those kids. If you're an artist, become a fisherman. Reel in everyone you can, and get them involved. If you're a martial artist, stretch your abilities and use your new skills to reach out to people; and again get them involved.

And instead of lining your pockets, line your walls with pictures of the people you helped and line your mind with the intention to do even more.

Never give up. Never give in. Endeavor not to lose touch with yourself or your art.

And always make a difference.

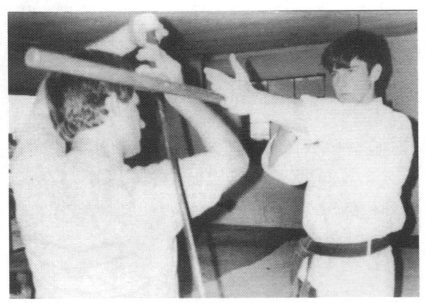

Left: Joe Fraley and Jeff Glaze practice a routine planned for a University play about the life of Musashi. The original play involved actors and fighters from local martial art clubs, raising local awareness about the arts.

Apples, oranges or painted potatoes?

Unfortunately most of the leaders of today's fighting schools are better marketing directors than they are teachers.

If they were good teachers, they would realize the damage they are doing to themselves and their chosen field of study, by trying to appeal to the masses.

I understand they are involved in a business, and that tailoring your approach to your intended audience is an important part of business, but to alter the original martial art to accomplish this is questionable at best.

It becomes disgraceful when in publications dedicated to these arts, there is more on marketing approaches than there is on improving technique.

Here's a free HINT:

• If you practice hard and don't worry about the marketing approach, the right people will come to you.

• If you start worrying about how you can draw more people into your school, you'll do exactly that – you'll draw all the wrong people. These will be the folks that will not want to work hard, will complain incessantly, expect to be graded even if their technique has not improved, and refuse to be involved with anything that doesn't directly benefit their own selfish selves.

For those who travel the second road, they may soon wonder why things have become so complicated. They'll wonder why their classes have become collection points for self-aggrandizing weenies. They'll have to ask themselves why they don't love what they're doing anymore. And worse of all, they'll have to start painting potatoes orange.

You see, many schools today have gotten far away from the original technique. Somewhere along the line, someone thought it would be better to do a technique a different way – perhaps because it looked better, or it worked better when practiced with music – or it didn't mess up their hair.

Anyway, this altered version was passed down to the next student, who was told "This is it. As it was given to me chiseled in stone by the Lord God himself!"

That student then passed the hopeless crap down again; and so on.

In the end, there's just a pile of mush. But it works great in demonstrations with Michael Jackson's "Bad" playing stoutly in the background.

So, now that Mr. Modern Day Martial Artist practices his technique, what was once a wrist grab and a specific strike, is now only a setup for a reverse punch, etc.

In short, nothing works very well.

This poor soul knows this, but he can still put on a good bluff, and he tells his students they can only practice amongst themselves. No outsiders are allowed to spar. Why? Because if that were to happen, he knows his squishy little punch and kick dance routine probably wouldn't work while he is lying on his back getting his face pounded in.

Subsequently, he seeks to control his student's exposure to outside students, because if his students should learn this, they may not be HIS students anymore. They may go elsewhere. Which means less money. Which means trouble paying the rent. Which means his painted potato technique is not being accepted as apples and oranges anymore. End of story.

Here's another HINT:

• Don't mislead people. If what you are teaching them is strictly an art – from an age when there was honor on the battlefield, then tell them that. Don't call it "effective street defense," because it's not – the last time I checked there was little honor in a street fight.

• If your method of fighting is to knock them down and pound them out – don't call it an art. It's not. There is little art to beating someone senseless; unless you consider the blood spatter pattern on the wall to be art. What you're doing is probably more of a method or science.

• If you're telling people they can break an arm or a leg with a technique; what's your basis for that remark? Have you ever done it? If you haven't, maybe you shouldn't open your mouth – or if you do, you should firmly place your foot in it.

• If you're making statements like "this will take down any opponent," you're an idiot. I have yet to see the technique that will do that – and if it exists, please someone teach it to me, then I won't need to train all the time. My first teacher, Donald Humes, once said that if you can take a pummeling and be completely unaffected, you don't need Karate – ie. Superman doesn't need the martial arts.

Committtment makes your life more worthwhile.

What's that smell?

You can't wade in crap and expect none of it to stick.

It seems that many martial art teachers believe they can go through their life collecting ridiculous fees for their lessons or seminars, turning down requests by people who can't afford to pay them enough.

Have you heard the word MERCENARY?

If you're not in it to help people, what are you doing it for? Collecting reasonable compensation for a days work is one thing; raping people is another.

Look at the history of the stuff you claim to be studying. Why were traditional martial arts developed in the first place? You will find that they were created for the protection of clan, family, home, palace or country. They were created for SERVICE. Once you remove SERVICE from the equation, all you have is organized brawling – or even worse; a Dance academy.

I'm not suggesting you shouldn't profit from what you do. I am saying you should give something back. There's plenty of causes out there, and very little money to go around.

Still, while most experienced martial artists are aware of these things, they choose to look the other way while their pockets are being filled. I guess they rationalize it.

"Well, look at Master DimYuk Sim," I can hear them saying. "He's collecting $5,000 for every seminar he does! We should be able to collect at least $6,000 for our seminars."

It is yet another sad state of affairs.

I recently heard that some teachers whom I had some great respect for, were collecting fees in this neighborhood, and turning down requests from organizations too poor to raise the same amounts of money. This is despicable. Remember, the only thing that makes a martial artist any better than a professional thug is SERVICE. If you can't be there for the people who need you – well, who are you there for? In the case of these two notable JuJutsu practitioners, they are obviously there for the people who have the most money.

If you look at the practice and employment of the martial arts as they were applied in the time and society of feudal Japan, you will see that the Samurai were the disciplined practitioners of the times. But their technique was applied in service to their lord. To remove the factor of service meant that a samurai was no longer retained. If he was not retained, he became a Ronin - a "wave-tossed man."

This was and is no place to be. Service should remain part of the equation.

All of us who have been teachers for a while have likely seen our share of disappointments - students who learned so much yet did nothing with their new skills. Students who showed promise, but never came back. Choices that once made, proved to be a mistake.

What I have come to believe, however, is that all is reasonable and all can be forgiven if the goal was "service."

We may not be able to satisfy or provide for everyone. We may not be able to make but a tiny ripple in the great sea of disappointment that is out there, but we can at least be there to try.

Where did the majority of the martial arts clubs / schools get lost then? It's not hard to find the place. Just follow the smell.

Martial arts dies and rots where someone who is respected takes advantage of others through the use of his skill. Do you think taking someone's money for a one-day seminar is wrong? What if you know the seminar will do them little good in the end? What if you know the technique they practice at your seminar they will forget as soon as they leave? Are you telling them they can learn everything they will ever need in a one day session. If so, let me know where that class is being held. I'll never have to practice again.

I'll boil all this down to a single question and a simple answer:

• What's the difference between taking someone's money for a course like this or holding them down and pulling it out of their pockets?

People who do this are a cheat. People who give nothing back are scum. People who do these things and think this doesn't apply to them, are fools.

End of sermon.

What's good technique?

Good technique for any artist, should be that place they always strive to reach, but never quite achieve.

I once heard it said that if you believed you had reached the top, you were misleading yourself. It is only a plateau.

I have never met a perfect person. I will never meet a perfect artist – and the only satisfied artists I'm aware of, are those who have painted their last picture.

Martial artists are the same. If you've reached a comfortable place, you took a wrong turn. The field of good technique bristles with construction signs. You are never the best you can be, but if you don't watch it, you might become the best you will ever be.

Don't ever be satisfied. Avoid contentment. Reach for perfection, but relish the fact that it will forever remain out of reach.

Repect

Students will look up to you. They will want to identify with you. Often they will go out of their way to help you. They will be overly respectful at times, fearful, etc. It is not right to encourage or take advantage of this.

I have visited teachers who encourage a yucky sort of relationship between their students and them. In situations like this, the student is overly dependent on the teacher and there is little growth possible for the individual. Some will say that we are in the business of teaching self-defense; others will say we are in the business of providing art instruction; others would say we are in the business of producing black-belts. I would say that we are not in business at all. Ours is a sacred duty – as everyone should have a duty – to help other people. Allowing respect to turn into something else is a disgusting, egotistical act – a thing which should be left to rock stars and soap opera queens.

Proper exercise and stretching is always necessary, and should be performed prior to every class. Here, Richard Ellis demonstrates some limbering exercises in Aikido.

Two additional wrist stretches used prior to traditional Aikido practices.

Creating change and allowing change

For everything there are seasons.

For plants, there is a spring, summer, fall and winter. For ideas, hopes and dreams, there is a beginning, middle and end, and for people there is Birth, Life and Death.

And within these circles there are other circles. For our students, there is a time when things are new, there is a time of discovery, and there is a time when they know they have received everything they need from you. To restrain a butterfly after its fantastic change has taken place means killing it – along with the possibility of future generations.

Yet, I have seen teachers cling to their developing students, using their abilities to promote their own aims, without regard to the student's needs or wishes.

If your job is to help them develop – once that has happened, you should let them go.

How do you know when this change has occured?

You won't. They will.

One day they won't come to practice, and that will be the beginning of something new.

This same idea applies as much to people who have trained with you regularly as to those who have only come to your class once. It may be that they only ever needed one visit to your dojo – maybe they needed more. Whatever the case, they came to the well, drank some water and left.

Incidentally, I'm not comparing us to the well – just the rocks that it is made of.

Associations

Do you belong to an association? Why?

There is strength in numbers – but strength to do what?

If you do belong to a larger organization and you pay regular dues to them, you should ask yourself some simple questions based on enlightened self-interest.

• Why did you join the organization, or why is your dojo a part of it?

• What are the goals of the assocaition? Are they goals you agree with?

• Does the association use its power politically?

• What causes does the organization support?

• Where does your money go? How is it used? Who benefits from it?

• Who is the head of the organization? Where do they live and under what conditions?

• What do you get from the organization that you can't do yourself?

Remember, you may have a reason for joining the organization – but someone else had a reason for starting the thing in the first place. If it was a good reason to begin with, don't you think it's your responsibility to make sure it's still a good reason, before you contribute your students' paychecks to it?

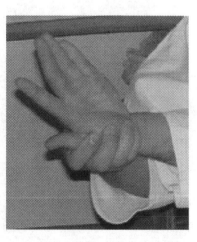

Show me the money

I once knew a teacher who sold out.

Actually, in one way or another, I've known many people who have sold out.

I've sold out, too. I've made compromises and adjustments to achieve goals – to be able to continue to make a difference.

When you're on a hunt for fame or fortune, there's little room for anything else. You can't help anyone if you're always helping yourself.

Examine your motives. Believe what you are thinking in the quiet moments. If at your center you feel guilt – if you don't believe in what you're doing; find out why, and fix it.

The bottom line is that selling out in itself is not a bad thing. Just be sure to sell out for something you believe in – not so you can be the biggest, coolest, meanest or best – just so when it's all over, you can look back and know that you did something that counted.

Child wonder

Everybody wants to teach a child wonder.

You've seen these kids – four feet tall and all dressed out with shiny new black belts. Now, belts may mean different things to different clubs, but it's probably not right to grade a child in the same way you grade an adult. They are after-all, a child. To expect them to have the same abilities, mentallly and physically, as an adult, is ridiculous. To train them as if they do, is dangerous. This is why Gichin Funakoshi developed his Karate-Do for children in the school system, and it's also why Jiggoro Kano put together Judo from Ju Jutsu.

Teaching and grading children should be a separate thing from that which is done for the adults.

Some teachers will have students regraded once they join the ranks of the adults. This is reasonable. Remember, although a samurai was initiated at the age of five, he was given wooden swords – not razor-sharp metal ones.

Something which should also be considered is the style of martial art the child is learning. I would submit for argument that children should first learn a whole-body art like wrestling or Judo – something to build their strength, discipline, coordination and reflexes. Following that, a study of Karate or Tae Kwon Do and lastly, an internal art like Kung Fu, Tai Chi or Aikido.

This is a good path for a young man or woman, and in my opinion, would develop a strong, flexible, tempered individual.

Ideas from the Old School

Another interview with Sensei Henry Ellis, 5th Dan

Beginners?

I must point out that it's very important for every student to realize that they were once beginners. We often see with students who have become very accomplished after just a few months that they forget that they were beginners and they don't treat new people with the same kindness that they were treated with. It's very important to help beginners along with just a few words of

encouragement and as they progress, they too will be able to take just a little more of the stresses and strains of practicing serious Aikido.

Color or Black and White?

As a martial artist for over 45 years, I still believe in the old Judo system of color grading. There is a lot of nonsense being propagated by these various organizations which do not approve of colored grading – everybody wears a white belt. Personally, I think there is nothing smarter than seeing a class line up in grade, with beginners at the back and the various grades leading to the front row and first kyu, with Sensei sitting at the front of the class. This is an incentive for the students to progress and become part of the next line and the next grade – this is called incentive and initiative. To take these colors away, takes these things away too. I've heard it said that some of these organizations believe that giving colors creates a system of egotism between students. This is all nonsense, as I have never seen this. I find it very frustrating when I visit dojos where all the students are wearing white belts. Because of the power of my technique, if I was to choose a student for demonstration who was a genuine white-belt, there may be a problem as I might injure that student with my technique. I just find this attitude totally stupid; and I do not approve of it.

Where's the teacher?

Coming back to this – when it comes to Dan Grades, only Dan Grades wear hakama – some years ago I visited a dojo and I was very impressed to be invited to this place as when I stepped on the mat, I saw so many people in hakama. I had never seen so many Dan grades at one seminar. So I congratulated the chief instructor at this organization at the amount of Dan Grades attending and he said "Oh, sensei, I must tell you, they're not all Dan Grades.

"Well," I said, "when you invited me here, you said you were true traditional Aikido. If you are traditional, why are you telling me now that you have people who are not Dan Grades wearing hakama?"

There must have been about 40 - 50 students wearing hakama.

So I said to all the students, "If you are black belt and are wearing a hakama, that's fine. But, anyone who is not a black belt and is wearing a hakama in three minutes time, will be treated by me as a Dan Grade."

Well, it was like a flash of lightning in every direction as students exited the mat and came back wearing their true colors. Once again, this is another aspect of devaluing true, traditional Aikido. Aikido is being eroded in many areas by this kind of stupidity, and these are the people who are eroding it and its principles; bringing it down from traditional Aikido to what is now, fantasy Aikido.

Respect

All students, once they join a dojo, are shown ettiquette, respect and discipline not only by the senior sensei, but by the assistants. And they too, without prompting, should show this respect to beginners when they join. It's important to encourage and help to build their own dojo. The sensei alone cannot do this – this has to be done with the help of every single student in the dojo. And every single student should help with the dojo – either by helping to advertise, cleaning; anything that helps the dojo is an important factor. Usually when a student reaches green-belt, he is then in a position to be made an assistant to a senior instructor.

Assistants

In traditional Aikido, it was always the assistant who made sure that his teacher was shown the utmost respect. For example, when Sensei Derek Eastman became my assistant in 1959, he would always carry my bag into the dojo. In fact, I did a seminar just recently. And you've got to realize that Mr. Eastman has been my assistant now for 40 years. Well, as we were getting our bags out of the car, Mr. Eastman suddenly grabbed my bag off me.

So I said, "Give that to me!" Because he had his bag and sword and bokken and jo in one hand. But he said "no sensei. I've always carried your bag, and I will never stop."

And he carried my bag into the dojo. That after 40 years. This proves to anyone that you cannot buy respect - you have to earn it. I earned Mr. Eastman's respect, and he earned mine, and we've been together now as teacher and student and as teachers together, for over 40 years.

A true beginner

This brings me to another point. Most students when they get to Dan Grade, they suddenly believe they are masters. First Dan to the Japanese means "beginner." Now you've got your black belt, now you are a beginner. To most Westerners when they get a Dan Grade, they believe they are a master. All of the sudden, they wish to leave their teacher and start on their own. They have no respect for their teacher – they leave them and they go off on their own and in their own direction. Every student, whatever grade he is, must have a teacher. Because once he hasn't got a teacher, he stops learning.

- Ellis

A story about etiquette

I'm going to relate a very true story which happened in 1967.

A couple of years ago, Arthur Lockyear, who is a correspondent for International Fighting Arts, asked me to do my life story for publication in the magazine, he asked me if he could ask a question.

He said, "The area that I come from has a lot of Dan Grades who were on a seminar where you were assistant to Chiba Sensei – and I've heard some serious stories about you, and I want to know if they are true."

What he asked me did in fact happen.

At this seminar, Chiba Sensei was in the dressing room and I was on the mat starting preparation. Sensei came out and called me over.

He said, "Mr. Ellis, these people in the North of England do not show the same respect that your dojos in the South of England show. Would you please talk to these people about ettiquette."

So I went back on the mat after assuring sensei that I would discuss ettiquette and discipline to these people.

I then asked everyone to sit down and said "from this point on, Chiba Sensei will not be referred to as Kazuo. He will only be referred to as Sensei or Chiba Sensei."

These people who'd been coming up and tapping Chiba Sensei on the shoulder and wanting to be friendly with him – well, one of them stepped forward and he said, "look, I work for an international company and I call my boss, Bill."

"But you're not with your company," I said to him. "You are now doing a martial art, and your Sensei is not your boss – he is your teacher. And, I am not interested in your personal situation. All I am saying to you is that from this point, you will not only call Chiba Sensei, "Sensei," but you will call me that as well. If anybody dares to call me by my first name, you will be responsible for your own problems that will result from that."

So this man said, "Well, I'm not going to call Chiba 'Sensei,' I'm going to call him 'Kazuo.'"

So I said, "Any man that does this – any man that shows the slightest disrespect, I'll drag off the mat and beat the living shit out of him in the car park. You all know I can do it; and you all know I will do it."

Although this story went around for many years afterward, I was most surprised after 30 years, when the correspondant for International Fighting Arts told me that this is something he'd heard.

I told him "Well, I can assure you that this is a true story, and that during the whole seminar which lasted for a week, we never had a problem."

If one observes a lot of teachers when they take a seminar – they try to create a new technique that has never been seen before – most of the time it is just a combination of movement that can ony be conducted between Uke and teacher that is rehearsed and worked together. I have seen this so many times with these conjured-up techniques. It's totally worthless.

Loyalty is bought with blood. Honor is simply about doing what's right.

When teaching a group of students at a seminar, you have to assess, as a teacher, the grade of all those students; and give them something they can take away and work on in the future. If you try to teach them something that is way above their head – they will have wasted their money, time and energy. I never do this. What I always do is teach strong, basic technique. And although we call it "basic," it is the groundwork for all technique; high grade and otherwise. Once a student has a good background in this, the rest will follow.

Teachers are teaching students techniques that are totally useless to them and will not help them with their future standard. They are far better teaching them strong basic.

For example: When we think of the Empire State Building – it used to be the tallest building in the world – and we always thought of it as a magnificent building. But without the foundations, you could never have reached the height of that building. And on the top of that building, there is a luxury penthouse. What is the value of that luxury penthouse if the foundations are weak and inferior?

-Ellis

How does practicing a martial art affect people

As long as good instruction is given, then all students will benefit. Many students have experienced the confidence they have gained from overcoming the anxiety felt when surrounded by strangers, handling problems with colleagues and family, and facing a physical confrontation.

If the training is effective, students work and help to improve each other. The Kyu grading system is very important in aiding this. Some students have a natural ability and will progress faster; however, the way of Budo is for the higher grade to encourage the lower to use all their strengths in techniques and attacks, whilst having the ability not to cause physical harm to the lower grade.

This system, as it progresses through the kyu grades enables all students to become strong practitioners.

The bully either quickly gains the self-confidence required not to bully and hurt those weaker, or leaves the dojo, not wishing to be confronted as the practice becomes harder amongst the more experienced.

Eastman

What do you consider your greatest accomplishment in Aikido?

I think that after first meeting Sensei Henry Ellis, 40 years ago, and then with his instruction, to be able to attain Dan grade; and now to still be training together and enjoying the practice – I consider that to be my greatest accomplishment in Aikido.

It gives me pride that both Sensei Ellis and myself had our Dan grade training certificates personally authenticated by Master Morihei Ueyshiba – I think this stopped after Number 500 was issued. Also a source of pride is the knowledge that the pupils we have taught and graded are a credit to the martial art of Aikido.

-Eastman

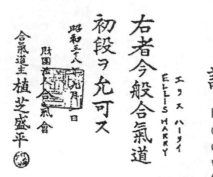

Left, one of the original Aikikai certificates which was presented in the 1960s to Henry Ellis.

To attempt to understand a method through anything other than hard practice is courting disaster. The classroom is a useful place to gain information, but at some point, it must be applied. Information is the circle, application the triangle.
And the box which contains both is you.

Where Aikido as a martial art is heading A general state of decline

I believe that there is now two distinct groups of people who profess to teach and practice Aikido. Those who wish to further Aikido as the martial art taught by Morihei Ueyshiba in his prime years, and those that only wish to practice harmonised movement of Aikido techniques and the Aikido gleaned from film and books of Morihei Ueyshiba in his later years.

At a recent seminar I was asked to teach basic Aikido technique. Afterwards many expressed the belief that I had been teaching a form of Ju Jutsu, because it was effective when being met with resistance by relative beginners.

I felt this was indicative of the way the martial art has been removed from the practice of Aikido by those instructors who are unable to effectively control, by technique, the very pupils they profess to teach.

There are instructors claiming to be 5th - 8th Dan Aikido – some having first trained with a traditional Aikido school, then leaving either to better their grade with a harmonised style, or start their own school. Either of these bear little relevance to the teaching of Morehei Ueyshiba.

Master Kenshiro Abbe taught that full competitive Judo should slowly be curtailed after 55 years of age as the body structure will start to weaken after this. This is also true of Aikido. But at no time should a strapping 12 to 35-year-old be taught to practice as a 70-year-old.

Those instructors who are able, must stress that Aikido is a true martial art and not a version of harmonised moving yoga.

It does sadden me to hear instructors alluding to be very close to Japanese masters who allegedly taught them, when they were in fact taught by teachers in their own country – whom they never mention.

The teaching we received was always to give respect to our senseis. More so, if eventually achieving a higher grade.

-Eastman

How does practicing a martial art affect people

As long as good instruction is given, then all students will benefit. Many students have experienced the confidence they have gained from overcoming the anxiety felt when surrounded by strangers, handling problems with colleagues and family, and facing a physical confrontation.

If the training is effective, students work and help to improve each other. The Kyu grading system is very important in aiding this. Some students have a natural ability and will progress faster; however, the way of Budo is for the higher grade to encourage the lower to use all their strengths in techniques and attacks, whilst having the ability not to cause physical harm to the lower grade.

This system, as it progresses through the kyu grades enables all students to become strong practitioners.

The bully either quickly gains the self-confidence required not to bully and hurt those weaker, or leaves the dojo, not wishing to be confronted as the practice becomes harder amongst the more experienced.

Eastman

What do you consider your greatest accomplishment in Aikido?

I think that after first meeting Sensei Henry Ellis, 40 years ago, and then with his instruction, to be able to attain Dan grade; and now to still be training together and enjoying the practice – I consider that to be my greatest accomplishment in Aikido.

It gives me pride that both Sensei Ellis and myself had our Dan grade training certificates personally authenticated by Master Morihei Ueyshiba – I think this stopped after Number 500 was issued. Also a source of pride is the knowledge that the pupils we have taught and graded are a credit to the martial art of Aikido.

- Eastman

On the subject of Ko-Kyu and Ki

Ki and Ko-Kyu are not often spoken about in the Ellis Schools of Traditional Aikido. This is because these principles are difficult, if not impossible to put into words.

Even the Founder of Aikido, Morehei Uyeshiba acknowledged this, and was heard to say once, "One cannot talk naturally about Ko-Kyu, and those who do so are liars."

Yet today, modern Aikido teachers tread fearlessly into this philosophical realm - offering up strange definitions for Ki and Ko-Kyu, stranger exercises for practicing and developing these principles, and even stranger demonstrations to show them at work.

In 1964, some nine years after Aikido was introduced to the West, Sensei Matsuharu Nakazono, then the Official Representative of the World Center Aiki Kai So Hombu, attempted to describe the undescribable in a British newsletter called The Judo News..

Nakazono related the fact that Ueyshiba himself believed the concepts of Ki and Ko-Kyu to be impossible to put into words.

"And yet I am trying to talk about it," wrote Nakazono. "It is Strange."

"But I must answer Mr. Naessens' (the interviewer) question. I will therefore, become a liar. Mr. Naessen's friendship makes me become a liar ..If you will understand this, I shall be happy."

Nakazono explained that the translation for Ko-Kyu is "to breath out-to breath in." He then explained that Ko Kyu to his understanding was a universal quality which could be manifest in the human body.

"Ko-Kyu is invisible, but manifests itself in many ways. Thus Master M. Uyeshiba had a physical strength to such an extent that it is impossible to conceive it scientifically. We have often talked with him about it, and we have understood that it is above all a case of spiritual power. His power was such that those who have not been able to realize it for themselves could have thought it was exaggerated. But all those, and there are many of us, who have seen and tried it, know that I am speaking the truth. I ask you to admit that there are extraordinary things. This power which the human body can produce is the power of Ko-Kyu which is the very basis of the practice of Aikido."

Nakazono pointed out in the article that Ko Kyu can exist in many forms. He used paintings as an example. Existing only in lines and colors, a painting still has the power to communicate powerful feelings. Nakazono suggested that this communication was really just the influence of the painter himself.

Ki is a separate idea from Ko-Kyu, and translates into "Universal Power."

In a later article in Judo News, Nakazono suggested that it was this "power" which creates life and movement.

"If it seems difficult for us to talk or to write about Ki and Ko-Kyu," said Nakazono, "Aikido will help us to discover the meaning of them because it is the very expression of these two principles."

-Rogers

Fantasy technique and living the fantasy

"What I have experienced – which is so common within Aikido," said Ellis, "– is the student/teacher who conveniently forgets all of his or her years of training with a Western teacher and instead claims they have been trained by the Japanese (perhaps after attending only a couple weekend seminars with a Japanese teacher).

"Although I was assistant and dedicated student to many Japanese masters who visited the U.K., I have never referred to any master as my "friend." I preferred to call myself a very priveledged student.

"For example, one article I read from a teacher in the Midlands, who was a regular student of Sensei Williams and myself, stated that Kenshiro Abbe Sensei and Chiba Sensei were 'great friends" of not only him, but also his wife. This man also states that Abbe Sensei was primarily a Judo master, who travelled extensively around the U.K. and Europe teaching.'

"I have no knowledge of him ever teaching Aikido outside of his dojo in Kings Cross or The Hut. Abbe Sensei's English was so poor that he had great difficulty in engaging in any kind of conversation with "his friends." When teaching, it would always be the same word – "necessary." "Necessary, this action" or "Necessary, that action. A slap with the shinai explained everything else.

I think these people who are creating fantasy histories, have very little history – so they are crying out for some credibility. Maybe that's where all these extra titles, grades and certificates are coming from."

"With reference to making up techniques; some years ago, when I was one of the instructors at the British Aikido Board's National Seminar at Brunel University, London, I saw the worst example of creating fantasy technique for the sake of it. This instructor lay on his back and told his uke to run forward and grab his big toe. As he took the big toe, he then made a superb high-flying ukemi. He was so pleased with this technique that he performed it several times with the same uke. I must point out that when he stood up, I expected him to laugh and show that this had been a joke. To my amazement, he was serious.

– Ellis

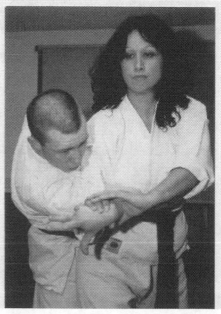

Above: Sensei Andy Lyons and Sensei Derek Eastman practice Jo technique in 1988.

Left: The first American-produced Dan Grade in the Ellis Schools is presented to Paul Emel in 2004.

Right: Sensei Ellis' first female assistant, Anita Wilson takes technique.

BODY

The practice of kata (static technique) is not a singular thing. It involves and requires the engagement of all the three aspects of the warrior. Without this, kata is an empty exercise.

A guide to the Ellis School Technique

**Illustrations by Dave Rogers
2nd Dan
Photos taken during practice in September 1999.**

1st Form Traditional Aikido

Katatemochi
(One hand to catch)

Diagonal wrist grab.

Note: where possible, dark and light colored uniforms have been worn so that the techniques can be seen more clearly.

Where the "form" system came from

I joined the first beginners class at the Hut in 1959. At this time there were no "forms" only the kneeling kata of Aikido.

Basic instruction was given by either catching same side (ie. Uke left to Nage right), Migi hamni, or from Shomen Uchi – a strike to the center of the head.

Masamichi Norro Sensei became representative of the Aikikai, being responsible for Europe and North Africa. Basing himself in Paris, France – a convenient center – he noted that the standard or level of European students had not developed evenly. Norro Sensei used the same nage waza or throwing techniques, but started with right to right (first form) as in a western handshake.

As the pupil learned the basic five throwing techniques: Shihonage, Kotegaeshe, Iriminage, Kaitenage and Tenchinage, along with basic principals in application and immobilization, they worked closer to the body (left to left, "second form"), then one hand gripping shoulder area (third form), then chest area (4th form). Through atemi attacks, rear attacks, two-hand attacks, etc., each way of being attacked or caught, the student learned the same basic throw, immobilization and application.

In this way, Norro Sensei felt it would be easier for himself to teach the various senseis to our standard.

Ken Williams Sensei welcomed this approach and Ellis Sensei taught this system as being the easiest approach to learning Aikido. The actual techniques remained the same as those previous to Norro Sensei.

-Eastman

Shihonage
1st Form

The technique should be taken with firm pressure on the joint of the wrist and good extension as you step into it.

First form should be practiced with strength, good form and balance. However, as with all the other technique, it should be practiced with movement and a feeling of movement. Static Aikido is dead Aikido. To learn to use any of it properly, a pratitioner must exercise dilligently and with some degree of resistance and speed. It cannot be performed like a robot – with choppy mechanical movement.

Seen above is the first of our techniques – Shihonage, as it is practiced from first form. The arrows represent direction – or in some cases, a feeling for the direction you should be moving. In no way are these to be considered as actual movement for the practitioner. To understand the performance of the techniques it is necessary to become a serious student and step onto the mat. There, with hard practice, all these things will become clear.

Kotegaeshe
1st Form

This technique counts on gently
building pressure throughout the
extension of the opponents arm. This
unbalances the opponent and allows
the technique to be placed easily on
the wrist.

Iriminage 1st Form

The arm should stay relaxed as the opponent attacks. After entering into the technique, the head of the opponent should be placed on your shoulder. A subsequent lead will unbalance them, then an entry into the technique will finish it.

Iriminage, 1st Form

With irimminage, in all cases, the important thing is to enter strongly. Think: shoulder to shoulder – head to shoulder – turn and take.

At this point, a choke can be applied, making the finish of the technique simply a case of stepping back and kneeling.

Tenchinage 1st Form

This is named "Heaven and Earth Throw" for a very good reason. The technique is accomplished by splitting the opponent's balance while at the same time, driving yourself into the space which the opponent is occupying. With proper extension and appropriate force, the technique can be acomplished. Application must be fierce and uncompromising. The opponent must first be taken before the movement is even begun. Without this, the end result will be less than anticipated.

Note: Tenchinage is an excellent gauge of spirit. Without spirit Tenchinage cannot work unless the opponent is cooperating, and allowing himself to be thrown.

Above: Tenchinage must be done with a stong cut and move-into the opponent at 100 percent. The cut and step with its subsequent extension should all occur at the same instant, splitting the weight and balance of the opponent.

When breaking away from the grasp of the opponent in tenchinage, you should be sure to turn your captured hand so that it may escape through the gap created by the thumb and forefinger of your opponent. Additionally, it may be necessary to use your elbow and body to break the grip. When this is accomplished, the left hand will cut and extend downward,

In the execution of this movement, force continues to build exponentially, until the eventual throw.

Entry on this technique is very important. It should be a steady, building force.

Kaitenage 1st Form

Kaitenage 1st form is again using a cut, followed by an entering motion into the gap which is created beneath the cut-away limb.

Here is the entering motion mentioned previously. The cut and entering as it is shown at left, should be accomplished by pushing the hips through the gap first. The body then follows.

The next part of this technique is a complete turn and control of the arm (elbow and shoulder). As shown below left, the position of the head of the opponent should be against your hip. A complete reversal of this position can then be executed taking the technique.

Ikkyo 1st Form

Ikkyo is affected by good extension and positive motion. Control on the wrist and elbow should be absolute. This is the only way to complete Ikkyo with success. By extending the attacking hand into the eyes of the opponent, then redirecting the elbow into an arm-bar, the technique can be accomplished.

The pin can be managed several ways, but it should be noted that a practitioner of Aikido can roll out of a pin unless his head and neck is immobilized.

Nikkyo is a good, positive technique, but it must be executed strongly with a feeling of cutting into the wrist. The figure at left has an exaggerated, high position on the arm. To execute this well, your hands should stay low — at your center.

Nikkyo 1st Form

Common mistakes in this technique include improper control of the hand, movement which is too relaxed, poor atemi, loss of the square made by the hand, arm and body, motion against the wrist which is too linear and extension which is also too linear. There is a distinct flow and timing to the execution of this techique. If this charactreristic cannot be felt, then the movement is wrong.

In sankkyo it should be remembered that when entering you should remain close to your opponent. If a piece of paper can be inserted between you – you're too far away. This tight turn will allow you to execute a strong and nearly indefensible atemi to the ribs. The resulting technique can then be made without difficulty.

This requires a tight turn into the opponents shoulder, an elbow strike low into the ribs, and control of the hand.

To make the technique work, positive control must be kept on the blade of the hand, so that it makes a square in relation to the rest of the arm. The throw will then work if the opponent is off-balance.

Sankyo 1st Form

The third principle of Aikido involves a powerful wrist turn in which tremendous forces are applied to the wrist elbow and shoulder joint. More than likely, this technique was originally intended as a complete destructive movement. It can, however, be turned toward control of the opponent. In traditional Aikido it is practiced with a pin or a throw, although in modern schools the throw has become more common. To accomplish sankyo, one must first turn the opponent's arm firmly against them. This can be done directly, or by turning underneath their arm. The technique can subsequently be accomplished by making a square with the opponent's hand and their arm. A wave-like motion is then applied to take the opponent backwards and off-balance. The throw, or an effective pin can then be applied.

Positive extension is equally as important here as it is on most of the other techniques.

There are those who would say that coordination of mind and body produces the third aspect; spirit. They are misled. Spirit comes from the continual firing of mind and body in the forge of combat. The true warrior is a combination of the coordinated aspects of mind, body and spirit. Spirit cannot breed mind, mind cannot breed spirit and body can only exist. The mother of spirit is trial, discomfort, diversity and pain. The warrior exists and is successful because all three aspects are in place and in coordination.

2nd Form
Traditional
Aikido

Katatemochi

(One hand to catch)

Straight-line
wrist grab.

Shihonage 2nd Form

Shihonage, 2nd Form

The take in this version of shihonage should be strong but smooth, starting from gripping the hand from beneath. Following this, a good, positive extension will give you your technique.

In second form Shihonage, the movement has not changed much from the first grouping. It is the entry into the movement that is different.

Kotegaeshe 2nd Form

The attack is second form is in many cases, met by a cutting motion at the wrist or arm. This cut should be strong, but not overpowering. You must be able to grasp the cut-away wrist following your turn. After this, an extension will bring your opponent's hand to your center where a turn of the hips will take him to the ground.

Iriminage 2nd Form

Here you can see the completion of iriminage as it is executed. The turn and control shown are correct, although the positioning is

exaggerated so that you may note hand position.

Iriminage is about triangles and diagonals. In order to break the opponent's balance, he needs to be tilted onto a corner – like a heavy box: it moves easiest hen it is tilted onto a corner.

Tenchinage 2nd Form

With tenchinage, 2nd form, you do not need to cut the opponent's hand away. A simple extension is all that is required to make the technique work.

Iriminage 2nd Form

Iriminage in 2nd Form requires good timing. You should be moving even as the opponent is coming toward you. In some cases, a small leap as you enter will give you a little better control.

In tenchinage it is important to have good, positive extension throughout the technique. As in First Form, the motion should be a steady increase of power into the throw.

Kaitenage 2nd Form

As in first form, the entry is at the elbow and forearm of your opponent. When making the enry, a tight turn around this limb leaving no room between the two bodies should be accomplished. Good positive control should be taken as you exit the turn and either extend for the throw or take the opponent to the ground..

The next part of this technique is a complete turn and control of the arm (elbow and shoulder). As shown below left, the position of the head of the opponent should be against your hip. A complete reversal of this position can then be executed taking the technique.

Ikkyo 2nd Form

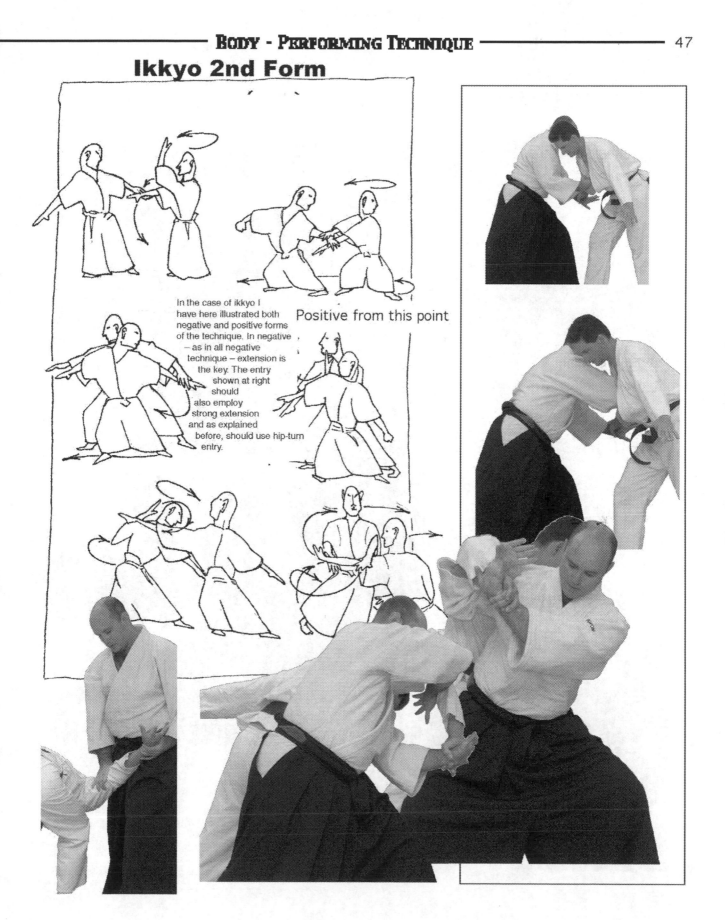

In the case of ikkyo I have here illustrated both negative and positive forms of the technique. In negative – as in all negative technique – extension is the key. The entry shown at right should also employ strong extension and as explained before, should use hip-turn entry.

Positive from this point

Nikyo 2nd Form

In 2nd Form nikkyo, two elements must be remembered. When taking this technique and entering, you must strike. This atemi will ensure the opponent's body is moving in the right direction so that positive control may then be established.

Nikyo can be a powerful technique if done correctly. Too often, however, it is not properly applied. A square must be maintained in the arm as it relates to the body, and the forearm must be parallell to the floor.

Sankyo 2nd Form

This version of sankkyo utilizes the same type of entry shown in ikkyo on the previous page. Again the cut and movement into the technique should be positive and the wrist and hand should be gripped and controlled at the base of the technique.

Although the aspects of
technique and resources are
crude by definition, they are the
foundation of motion in combat,
and subsequently require study
and respect.

3rd Form
Traditional
Aikido

Ryotemochi

(Two- hands catching)

Technique performed
as opponent
attempts to prevent
the drawing of the
sword.

Demonstrated by Dave Rogers, 2nd Dan
Ellis School USA Headquarters

Shihonage 3rd Form

Figures one through four represnt the initial movements for all third form techniques.

The movements are extremely exagerated here so that the basic patterns can be understood.

Here begins the first of the 3rd form techniques. Naturally it can be executed with or without a sword. All the basic tenets of control and extension still apply.

With 3rd form Shihonage, a good entry is paramount as you have to push against both of your opponent's arms in order to be able to get in and take the technique. As with many other third form techniques, the weapon is coming back into the opponent at the end.

Kotegaeshe 3rd Form

The same powerful entry with the sword is used for
Kotegaeshe as it is for Shihonage. When turning back into your
opponent to take the technique, the weapon is thrust against
your opponent's face and neck.

Kotegaeshe, 3rd Form

Shown as it would be
performed after the initial
four steps are completed.

Iriminage 3rd Form

Some important things to remember when performing this technique are to keep close, strong contact with the opponent; move into him – don't try to pull him into you; extend your trailing arm, whether or not you have trapped his beneath it. Some things to look for are a stong, balanced stance all the way through the motion; a positive mental attitude, looking your direction and extension

Remember, the motion is still powerful. Think about driving the weapon into your opponent.

Tenchinage 3rd Form

In tenchinage, entry is everything. What's shown below in the photographs is a negative entry to the technique. For a positive motion, the sword would be drawn into the face of the opponent as it is done for ikkyo.

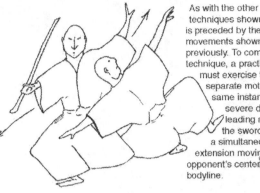

As with the other techniques shown, this one is preceded by the initial movements shown previously. To complete the technique, a practitioner must exercise two separate motions at the same instant. One is a severe downward leading motion with the sword hand and a simultaneous upward extension moving from the opponent's center his bodyline.

Kaitenage 3rd Form

In this illustration, as can be seen below, there is no pin, but of course, kaitenage can still be applied with a finishing technique. Important here is contact, control and good extension.

With kaitenage, the circle which is apparent in some of these techniques, gets bigger. It turns around the opponent's entire body. It is useful to note that the arms do not need to be gripping your opponent at the end of this technique, but if they are in the correct position, it will work as it should.

Ikkyo 3rd Form

With ikkyo, the weapon is definitely smashing upward into your opponent's face. As his elbow becomes visible, it is taken forward in a positive thrusting movement, until the arm bar is achieved. Your arms should remain relatively straight when executing this motion.

Nikkyo 3rd Form

Both of these techniques are shown withblades. But as with the other techniques in this form, they can be performed with or without weapons. In both of these thechniques, the act of cutting and extending is most important.

This version of nikkyo is shown extremely positive. Instead of turning away, we've cut directly into the opponent's face. Perhaps the early versions of this allowed for the smashing of the hilt of the weapons against the opponent's face – in any case, the handle of the sword is then used as an unyielding lever to take nikkyo.

Sankyo 3rd Form

Shown here are the last two of 3rd Form's eight techniques. It is important to stress the pushing through of the hips. In sankkyo, the hand is gripped at the bottom of the technique. The finish can be the destruction of the limb or a pin.

In sankyo, early control of the limb is important. If you can take the wrist as you are passing through the body, the technique will end appropriately.

Remember sankyo from other forms? It doesn't really change in third form. If you compare the picture at right to the one at left, you can see how the sword is still employed while controling the opponent's limb.

It's said that the moment a box is opened determines its contents – that until that moment, what's inside exists only as probabilities. In combat, probabilities exist because the warrior creates them. The way of the warrior is intent. Retreat or redirection are possible and useful tools, but should always be followed with a powerful entry. Success or failure is unimportant – the only item of importance in the moment of attack is the entry – all that is alive in that moment is the cutting edge of the sword.

4th Form
Traditional
Aikido

Gedan-mochi

(Grasping centerline attack.
The traditional version calls for
grasping the belt knot)

Demonstrated by Jeff Glaze, 1st Kyu
Ellis School, U.S. Headquarters

Shihonage 4th Form

Fourth form is taken from an attack in which the opponent grabs somewhere centerline on the body.

When taking 4th form, it should be noted that the back of the head is used to brace against the arm as you're passing through your opponent. Good positive control should be maintained on the wrist and elbow all the way through.

Kotegaeshe 4th Form

In kotegaeshe, the cutting motion in conjunction with the turning of the captured wrist will break the grip of the attacker and allow his wrist to be taken for use in the technique. It is important to remember to turn and extend deeply. At the finish the hips must turn!

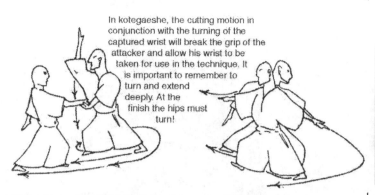

With kotegaeshe, the beginning is the same as it was for Shihonage, however, the gripping arm can either be cut away, or remain in place to take control. In this case it is shown with the opponent's arm being cut away, then the associated turn; and finally the control on the wrist.

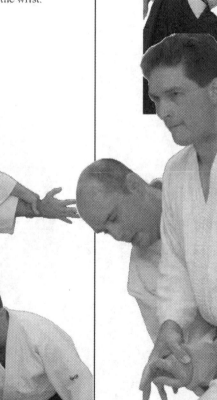

Iriminage 4th Form

With iriminage 4th Form, it is not entirely necessary to cut the attacking limb away. It's perfectly fine to leave the hand where it is. It is however, strictly necessary to extend properly and move through at 100 percent.

Of course, in iriminage, the entry is vital, but also vital is a good lead away from the body. As your opponent is in the base of this turn, he is unbalanced and can easily be taken by turning back into him. What helps with this technique is to realize that the attacking hand need not go anywhere. It can stay attached while you redirect your opponent.

Although your arm which extends past your opponent's head seems to have little purpose, it can provide an effective defense, once your opponent is thrown.

Tenchinage 4th Form

Note the direction of the extension in these graphics. Without this kind of extension, tenchinage will never work properly.

In 4th form Tenchinage, little attention should be payed to the fact that the opponent is grabbing hold of you centerline. As with every form of tenchinage, the response is nearly preemptive as it is timed exactly to the moment your opponent begins to move. The resulting motion is explosive and does not take into consideration the opponent's position. You split their balance on entry and extend straight through them.

BODY - PERFORMING TECHNIQUE

Kaitenage 4th Form

When turning through your opponent, you should concentrate on pivoting your hips through the gap created by opening up his attacking arm. In fourth form, however, it is unnescessary to open that gap with a cut. Instead, leave the attacking hand in place and turn through the arm. This will place you in an ideal position to finish the technique.

Ikkyo 4th Form

Ikkyo 4th form generally requires the same type of entry as Kaitenage 4th form. The pressure into the arm and against the opponent's body should be tight and strong. The pivot around the attacking limb should be fast but controlled. Lastly, control on the exit of the technique, which is placed against the opponent's elbow, should be very positive with a complete grip and not a forearm or a blade of hand control.

Nikkyo 4th Form

With Nikkyo 4th form, the executor of the technique should first step out of line of the attack., then taking the hand as shown above, should step forward with a punch, crossing over the captured limb.

Above and right shows the sequence as the technique is taken. In this step, it is important to take the opponent's balance, but keep pressure on the arm. When finally controlling the opponent's limb with nikkyo, you should make sure to keep their forearm horizontal with the ground as you apply pressure.

Sankyo 4th Form

For the finish of sankkyo in this form, 1st form or 2nd form, the posture and execution is identical. Once again, the practitioner should concentrate on the control of the elbow as they pivot underneath the arm. Later, positive control of the hand and wrist must be maintained to make a throw or pin.

Left it is possible to see the kind of control necessary to effect Sankkyo. The practitioner's hands firmly sandwich the opponent's hand. Your arms at this stage should be held close to the body and the throw should be accomplished with the entire boy moving forward into it.

Breath is nourishment for the three aspects. As we breathe
our mind expands, or body replenishes and our spirit
stretches. Breath in combat is taken in during the spaces
and expelled during defense or attack. To have poor rhythm
gives the opponent opportunity.

5th Form Traditional Aikido

Shomen-uchi

(Attack to center
of head - or
centerline cut.)

Demonstrated by Professor Henry Ellis
5th Dan, Head of the
Ellis Schools of Traditional Aikido

Shihonage 5th Form

As the attack for 5th form is straight in, shomen, the defense is either to step straight back as in the drawings at top, or to move directly in as shown in the photographs.

In these photographs, shihonage is presented in positive (omote) form. The attack in 5th form is shomen, and the defense can be made against empty hand or any weapon moving in this manner.

Important points to notice here, however, is the strong posture evident in figure one and two, the atemi in figure two and the straight back of figure three.

At left is a graphic depiction of the same technique, although this is shown in negative (Ura).

In this version of shihonage, timing is very important. The individual accepting the attack should move proactively - almost exactly at the same time his attacker does. This allows him the ability to control the situation and choose the action instead of trying to react to it.

With 5th Form the attack is coming from above in a straight line. To defend it, it is first necessary to step back away from the attack. The lead arm is then directed and grasped.

When entering, as with all forms of Shihonage, the body must remain tight to your opponent. Control remains firm on the wrist.

Turning away from the attack, the
opponent's wrist can be taken.

Kotegaeshe 5th Form

Once gripped, the
wrist can then be
turned inward for
the finish.

In 5th form the attack is
shomen (centerline cut to the
head). To take kotegaeshe it is
necessary to turn away from
the attack and lead the
extending arm in
an arc until it
reaches center.

Kotegaeshe
from shomen
directly relates
to defense
against a
descending
sword cut.

To avoid the
cut, the
individual
being attacked
must first turn
out of the
way. This turn
places them
back-to-back
with their
opponent -
and allows

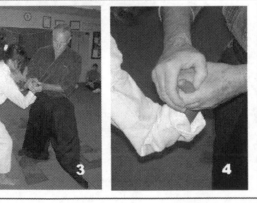

them to redirect the opponent's attack in order to take
the technique at the wrist. An important point here is to
extend outward and downward as shown in figure 2.
Another important point is to place your hand completely
on top of your opponent's - and not just use your thumb
to apply the pressure. The placement of your hand in this
way will allow all your body weight to be applied to your
opponent's wrist.

Iriminage 5th Form

Iriminage in 5th form is another major timing issue. As your opponent is moving into you for the attack it is necessary that you

For fifth form, the entry is directly opposing the attack, straight into the opponent. With iriminage, the technique is led around in a circle until the finish.

already be moving. In fact, if both individuals were weilding swords, the weapons of each individual would raise at seemingly the same time with the defenders blade extending towards and past the attacker (figure 2). As the defender turns into the attacker and leads their weapon toward the ground in a downward spiral, the attacker's balance is disrupted and it is possible to drop them easily to the ground for a control technique. The technique requires good contact with the attacker - if there is enough space to fit a piece of paper between the two individuals they are too far apart.

Another useful point is the control of the wrist and the head as illustrated in figure 4. These parts of your opponent should be carefully controlled - loss of either one would be disasterous.

IRiminAge 5th Form

Try to come into your attacker deep enough that your shoulders will be touching.

Always look your direction as you are making your turn. Although not shown here, you should place your attacker's head onto your shoulder and keep it there.

extend

step in

Tenchinage 5th Form

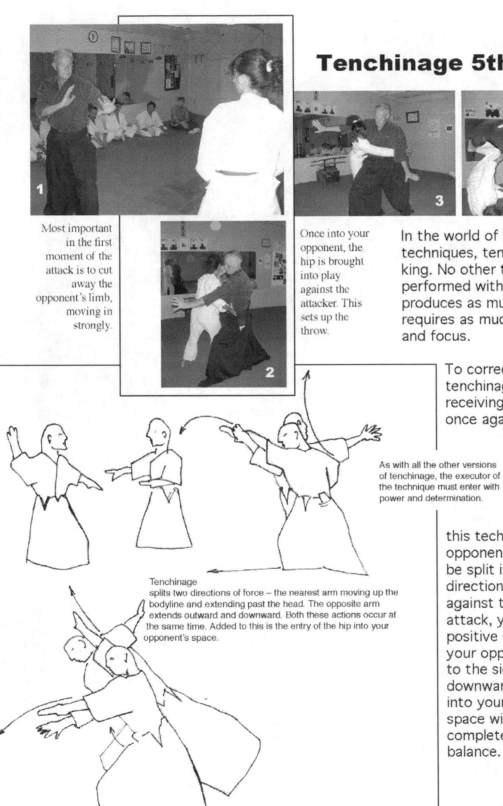

Most important in the first moment of the attack is to cut away the opponent's limb, moving in strongly.

Once into your opponent, the hip is brought into play against the attacker. This sets up the throw.

In the world of positive techniques, tenchinage is the king. No other technique performed within Aikido produces as much force or requires as much determination and focus.

As with all the other versions of tenchinage, the executor of the technique must enter with power and determination.

Tenchinage
splits two directions of force – the nearest arm moving up the bodyline and extending past the head. The opposite arm extends outward and downward. Both these actions occur at the same time. Added to this is the entry of the hip into your opponent's space.

To correctly execute tenchinage, the individual receiving the attack must once again move at nearly the same time as his opponent. To be able to execute a throw with this technique, your opponent's balance must be split in two different directions. As you enter against the shomen attack, your own very positive cut is shoving your opponent's attack to the side and downward - a simple step into your opponent's space will then completely take his balance.

Kaitenage 5th Form

In kaitenage, the important points to remember are the extension against the opponent's limb as you enter the cartwheeling motion, but also, there are atemi as seen in figure three and figure five. Keep good control on the arm and at the back of the neck.

As the attacker moves in with their cut, the defender is also moving to the outside. The turn the defender subsequently makes places their arm in line with the attacker's offending limb. A cartwheeling motion follows.

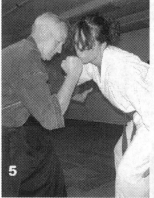

On the throw, keep a strong posture and extend forward as you step forward and into your opponent.

For kaitenage to be effective, once again, the entry into the technique must be strong. The attack can be met directly, or by leading the opponent's attacking arm.

The pivot point of the technique is your own arm where it contacts the arm of your opponent. As you turn through the end motion of this technique, your palms remain facing upward through the pivot.

Ikkyo 5th Form

In ikkyo 5th form, the attacking arm is once again intercepted – this time being thrust backward into the opponent. Control is then taken on the arm at the elbow (no open hand, blade of hand or wrist control of the elbow. It is gripped firmly.)

Important points to remember when executing this version of ikkyo is that you must move strongly into your opponent as the attack is initiated. Following that entry, good control of your opponent's elbow must be achieved. This is best done by gripping the elbow with your hand and extending the elbow into the side of your opponent's head - as if you were placing the elbow inside their ear. After rotating the arm forward, positive control is achieved.

stepping back

Your arms must not buckle as you enter into this arm bar. They should remain straight as you move in with your hips. The opponent is taken neatly to the ground.

Nikkyo 5th Form

The same entry is used here with the strike to the lower stomach area, then control.

Once again atemi is used as entry is made into 5th form nikkyo. The movement is positive as you are moving against your opponent's cut.

Note the positive control of the elbow as in ikkyo.

On the entry you should also be concerned with taking your opponent's balance and breaking down his posture.

Control as shown in figure four is kept tight to the body with the back of the opponent's wrist braced against the body. Torque against the joint is applied as the defender steps into the attacker's space and takes them to the ground.

The defense is positive, becoming its own attack. The attacker's limb is met as it begins, and it is turned inward to take sankkyo.

Notice that the entry is your own complete cut against your opponent's cut. A simultaneous strike to the kidneys should reduce any developing contest of strength or will and allow you to finish the movement.

Sankyo 5th Form

The entry for sankyo 5th form is identical to the entry for nikkyo. As you enter your opponent's space with your own cut, an atemi to the low center, starts the technique (figure 2). Following a turn, your inside arm is able to reach forward to grasp your opponent's wrist and hand. The grip should be secure and supported by your outside hand underneath (figure 4). Important points in this technique are similar to those in the application of nikkyo. The posture should be on-balance and strong.

However, the grip of the wrist is different in this technique and requires a much different application. when engaging control of the opponent, the direction of the torque should be slightly upward and rearward in an almost wave-like motion.

Note the change of hands at this point.

Extension into the attack should be very positive. This entry is used for both sankkyo and kaitenage as well as versions of ikkyo.

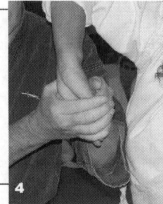

The grip here is important. Notice how the opponent's hand is positively sandwiched between your own.

Warriors are created on the mat, but only
teachers will remain or return there.
Warriors can't concern themselves with the
instruction of others, as they must be
continually focused on the mortal task they
were created for. When the warrior is forced
into improper molds, the spirit suffers.

6th Form
Traditional
Aikido

Yokomen-uchi

(Attack to side
of head.)

Shihonage 6th Form

In sixth form, the attack has changed from shomen to yokomen. Subsequently, the application of many of the techniques begins with the otward step illustrated in figure two. With shihonage, this outward step is accompanied by a strike to the side of the head (figure 2). Following that strike, the defender's hands meet at the wrist of the attacker, and the technique is then taken with an extension into the opponent and against the joints of the wrist, elbow and shoulder.

This example of shihonage is being shown with a pin, although it can obviously be taken as a throw. Important is the good control and the entry of the elbow, as shown in frome four.

The entry (attack and initial defense) for 6th form is pictured here in these first two drawings. All the techniques are then applied following these basic movements.

The attack must be firm to ensure your partner is under pressure to execute an effective technique.

Make sure to enter with power and control, so that if your opponent is coming in fiercely, you can still make the technique.

Kotegaeshe 6th Form

The motion is oblique for 6th form, placing you somewhat out of harm's way. But it is important to remember that you must attack at the same time, cutting to the temple. With kotegaeshe, a cut and lead is then applied to place you in the appropriate position to take the technique.

Once again, the opponent's attacking limb is redirected albeit softly, as shown in figure three. Following that motion, the hand and wrist is gripped and the technique is taken.

Make sure your grip is strong and you have positive control of the wrist.

Once again the good, positive entry into the technique with a strong, oblique response.

Keep hips level and shoulders in-line with hips. A good, positive turn with the wrist kept at center will ensure that the technique will be on.

Iriminage 6th Form

After the initial entry, the lead should be deep and strong. As you turn into the end of the technique, your hips should turn in-line with your shoulders and your elbow which is keeping your opponent's head into your body, should drop.

Two methods for doing iriminage 6th form are shown here. In the graphic, it's been simplified to a very basic form, while a more advanced version is described below.

Once again, the strike to the temple is evident, followed by a redirection of the hand, wrist. and arm of the opponent.

Then another entry into the opponent.

Note here, the control of the neck and chin.

Tenchinage 6th Form

In tenchinage – any form; the operative word is "enter." In order for the technique to work at all, the entry must be 100 percent, the extension through the body must be positive and overwhelming.

Tenchinage, the "heaven and earth throw," should be remembered for its name. When entering into the technique, the balance is being split two ways. The lead arm cuts away the attack, redirecting the opponent's attacking limb to the rear.

In the end of the technique, just prior to the throw, the hips come into the opponent.

Kaitenage 6th Form

In this 6th form technique pictured below, the technique is continued in spiraling circles until its conclusion.

After stepping oblique, redirect the opponent as in kotegaeshe. Then, opening the body up, pass underneath the outside arm (as shown at right). Once passing underneath the arm, kaitenage is done as usual.

Ikkyo 6th Form

Again, two different versions of a technique are shown. In the drawing, it is explained that an immediate entry into the attacking arm can take technique. A more complex form is shown below with atemi.

Note the grip on the elbow.

Take positive control on the other side of the arm.

Enter strongly and pivot around the arm.

Nikkyo 6th Form

Note the gripping of the wrist as it is pulled against the body. Also note the position of the forearm. It is parallell to the floor.

After stepping oblique in 6th form, you should grasp the wrist; and punching back into your opponent's face, turn the hand over and brace it against your body. Control is then taken with the opposite hand.

Sankkyo 6th Form

Once again, the oblique movement of the attack is matched by your own defense – turning outward, away from your opponent's motion.

Observe the change of grip.

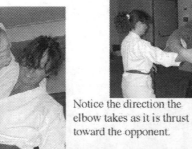

Notice the direction the elbow takes as it is thrust toward the opponent.

As with ikkyo, the entry is very strong with an associated pivot around the arm. When the technique goes on, the force against the wrist will lift your opponent off their feet.

When any of the three aspects are out of
balance, the other aspects will suffer for it.
Once integrated, mind, body and spirit can
no longer be separated.

7th Form Traditional Aikido

Chudan-Tsuki

(Punch or linear
attack to center)

Shihonage 7th Form

On this version of shihonage, it is most important to step back and away from the attack. The wrist can then be grasped and forced back toward your opponent. You must remember as in the illustration below right, to enter into your opponent with tight control.

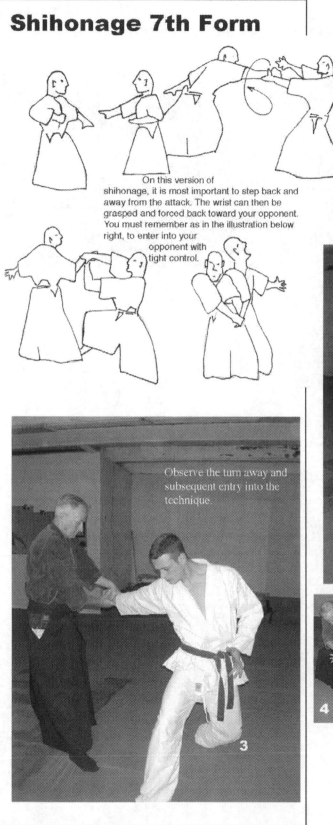

Observe the turn away and subsequent entry into the technique.

Notice that the entry is deep, and the control on the arm is complete.

Kotegaeshe 7th Form

With 7th form kotegaeshe, it's necessary to turn completely away from the attack, allowing it to pass you; then redirecting it into your centerline so that you can turn into the wrist. Remember, your hand must cover theirs.

When the punch comes in, the turn away is timed so that the technique can be applied, redirecting the punch so that the wrist turn can be applied.

Iriminage 7th Form

On this technique, the attack is allowed to pass by the body so that the technique can be led to its conclusion.

With iriminage, 7th, the method is similar to iriminage 5th. As the attack is being made to the body's center, the defense in this case is to step in – extend through a turn. Control is maintained as pictured below left.

Tenchinage 7th Form

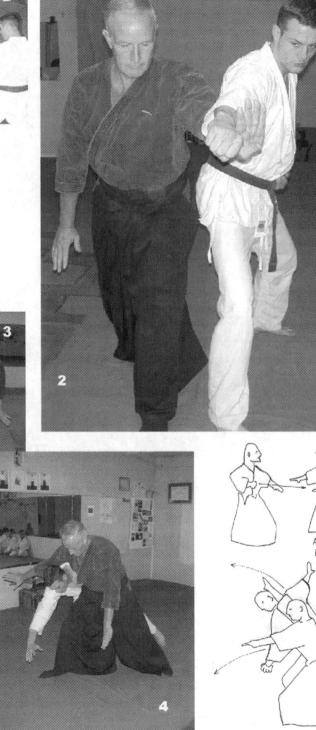

Again, the hips step through on this technique

As the punch comes in, sweep the arm away and enter into the technique before the attack has a chance to gain speed. Cut the attacking arm downward and away — entering into the body firmly with your hip. Step across and into your opponent deeply.

Kaitenage 7th Form

As you enter underneath the window you've created by knocking the attack down and away, you should be concentrating on pushing your hips through. After the hips are through, then the rest of the body follows.

Note the strike to the side of the head as the technique is entered.

The hips must turn strongly to finish the technique.

Ikkyo 7th Form

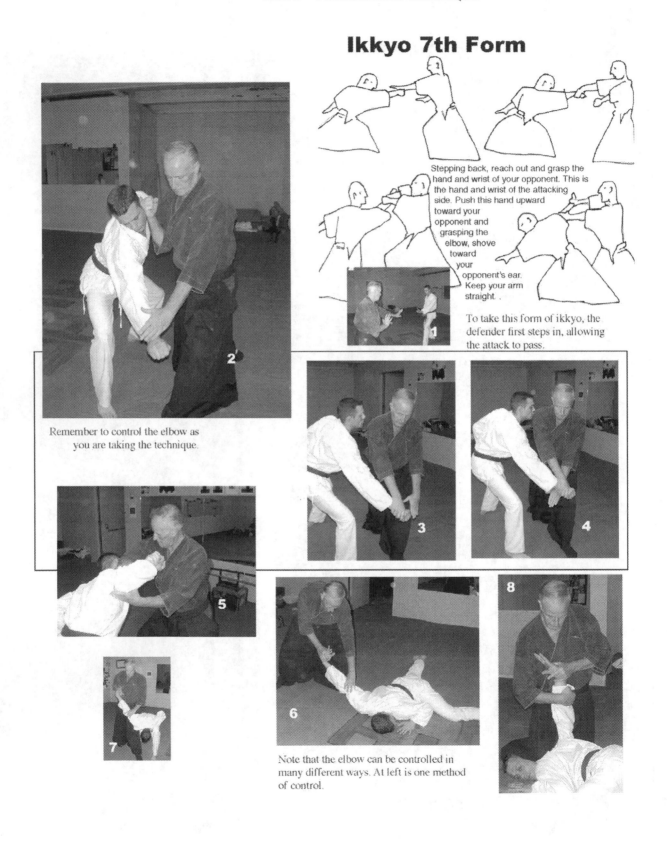

Stepping back, reach out and grasp the hand and wrist of your opponent. This is the hand and wrist of the attacking side. Push this hand upward toward your opponent and grasping the elbow, shove toward your opponent's ear. Keep your arm straight. .

To take this form of ikkyo, the defender first steps in, allowing the attack to pass.

Remember to control the elbow as you are taking the technique.

Note that the elbow can be controlled in many different ways. At left is one method of control.

Nikkyo 7th Form

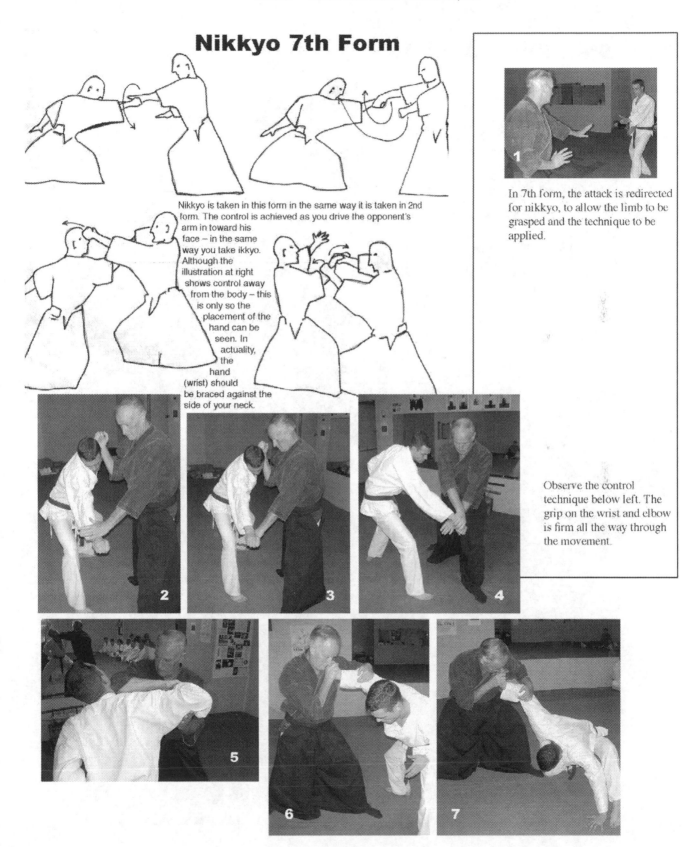

Nikkyo is taken in this form in the same way it is taken in 2nd form. The control is achieved as you drive the opponent's arm in toward his face – in the same way you take ikkyo. Although the illustration at right shows control away from the body – this is only so the placement of the hand can be seen. In actuality, the hand (wrist) should be braced against the side of your neck.

In 7th form, the attack is redirected for nikkyo, to allow the limb to be grasped and the technique to be applied.

Observe the control technique below left. The grip on the wrist and elbow is firm all the way through the movement.

Sankkyo 7th Form

Enter into the technique by moving quickly and firmly into your opponent, passing underneath the attacking arm. As you turn through, grasp the limb nearest you by the hand and wrist. Apply control by turning the hand inward and upward into yourself while keeping your opponent's forearm in-line with the centerline of your body.

Again with 7th form sankkyo, the defense includes a strike to the side of the head. The control soon follows, allowing the technique to be ended with a pin as in ikkyo.

When practicing a martial art, many students and
teachers will concentrate on technique or spirit as
individual areas requiring separate work. This is not
so. The proper practice of technique will develop spirit
as it tests the minds and bodies of the participants.

8th Form
Traditional
Aikido

Ushiro-tyotedori
Ushiro-ryokatadori
Ushiro-katatedori katate-kubijime

Shihonage 8th Form

Step back, projecting upward and opening a window to step beside your opponent. Grasp the outside wrist and turning it, step deeply into your opponent.

8th form technique is all about turning back into your opponent. Instead of concentrating on breaking your opponent's grip, you should use their grip to better effect the technique.

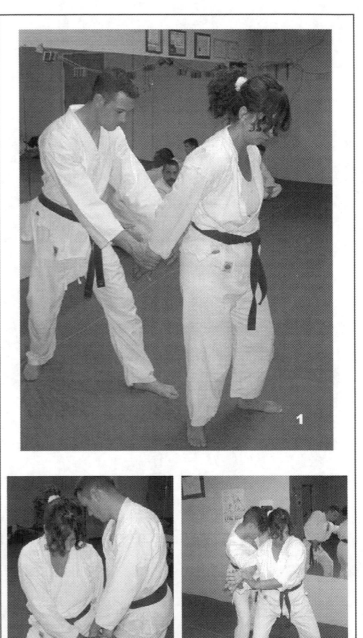

As you turn through, a strike to your opponent's face is made – as shown below. Then the technique is applied.

Kotegaeshe 8th Form

Step back against your opponent and open up a side of his body which you can step through. Then turn and cut your inside arm free. Another turn will place you in position with your back to your opponent. While leading him, extend outward and around, oblique. A third turn will place you in a position to more adequately apply a twisting motion against the wrist.

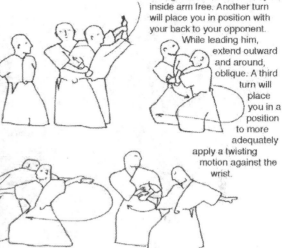

...shows a large gap between uke and nage, there should be little or no space between the two of you as you pass through the gap.

Iriminage 8th Form

Once again, turn in and cut away the opponent's inside hand. Then enter firmly and make a positive turn away from the direction you are both facing.

Once you've made this turn, you can then pivot your hips and take your opponent.

Tenchinage 8th Form

When providing the attack during practice, it should be a firm grip on your opponent's wrists.

Although the drawing at right shows the man placing his left (outside) hand high on the back, the actual position for an effective technique is low – at the small of the back, on the outside hip. Projection is then made by stepping firmly and deeply into your opponent's space.

The turn and step through is followed closely by a step back into your opponent.

Kaitenage 8th Form

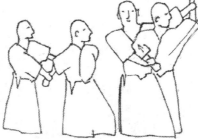

By cutting away the opponent's gripping arm, you can then turn into him and take control on the shoulder, neck and back. This is done by taking control of the outside arm, bracing yourself against your opponent's neck. A throw is done by pivoting to face the opposite direction while in this position.

On 8th form technique, the elbow strike to the body shouln't be forgotten. Following that, for kaitenage, the opponent's arm is led toward the floor, then brought up to control or throw.

Ikkyo 8th Form

Once again, step through the window opened at your opponent's side. Grip his wrist and turn it over, driving it into the side of his head or face.

1

2

3

As you turn into the body of your opponent, you must take immediate control of the opponent's elbow.

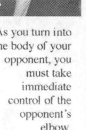

4

5

6

Nikkyo 8th Form

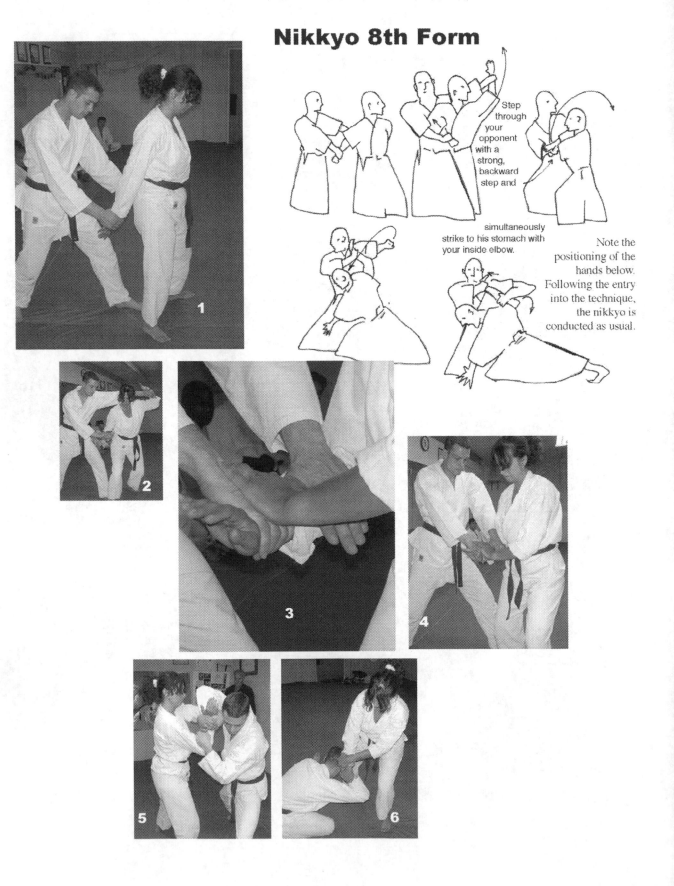

Step through your opponent with a strong, backward step and simultaneously strike to his stomach with your inside elbow.

Note the positioning of the hands below. Following the entry into the technique, the nikkyo is conducted as usual.

1

2

3

4

5

6

Sankkyo 8th Form

Keep positive control of
your opponent's wrist as
you turn in this technique.

Beginner's Checklist

How to wear a gi
A gi should be worn with the pants drawstring knot in the front of the body, and the jacket folded left side over right. The obi (belt) should be wrapped twice around the body with the widest section at the small of the back.

How to tie a belt
The obi has two main methods for tying. The first knot which is shown is the knot used by most martial arts clubs today. It characteristically flares the two belt ends outward and away from the knot.

The second knot is the old-style judo knot which is no longer used, but which offers the benefit of not coming undone as easily as the new knot.

How to bow
A bow is executed to show respect for your training partner, teacher or practice area. It should be executed so that at its deepest part, your body makes a right-angle and you show your opponent the top of your head — this is great respect. To bow at less of an incline, or to keep your eyes on your opponent as you bow may mean you do not trust him, or think less of him.

Right: The knot currently used by most martial art schools.

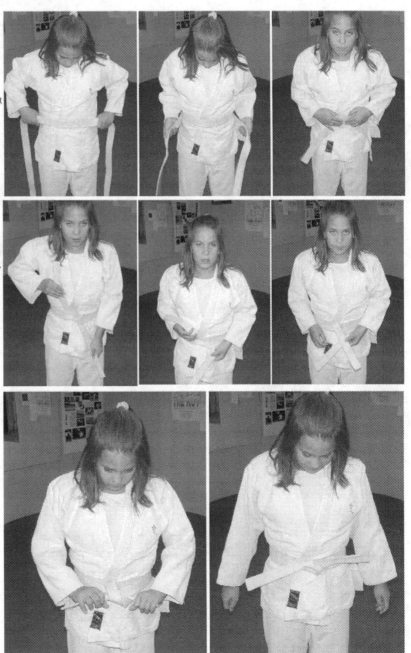

How to enter and leave the mat

When coming into the dojo, shoes should not be worn unless it is allowed by the school. Many dojos require that shoes for everyone be removed at the door before entering. This is done as a sign of respect, but also to keep the practice area clean. Also when entering, the martial art student should always bow to the center of the training area before proceeding inside. Do a standing bow to the dojo's center before stepping foot on the mat. If you have not been asked on the mat, you should remain seated properly at its edge until Sensei calls you out, or indicates that it is OK for students to begin warm up on the mat. When this occurs, it is considered good etiquette to do a seated bow to center again, before standing and coming on to practice. The bows to center may be exchanged for a bow to the kamiza (usually a little table centrally located in the dojo and displaying photos, weapons or other items). The kamiza is considered the place of the highest moral standing in the dojo, and is usually where photos of the old teachers will be displayed.

When leaving the mat, the student should again do a seated bow at the edge of the tatami and then a standing bow before stepping off. Before leaving the dojo, a final bow is also executed to the room.

When class is begun, all will line up in grade and sensei will turn to the kamiza to execute a formal bow to the school's logo, flag orrepresentative items, as well as showing that he is ready to proceed in the traditions of the teachers which have come before him and who's pictures reside on the kamiza or the wall around it.. Then sensei will turn back to the class and execute a bow to his students. This process is again repeated at the end of class and can include a seated bow between Sensei and his assistant - or the other dan grades on the mat.

In some clubs three claps are executed before making the bow to begin class and again before making the bow to end class. These claps take their origin in Shinto belief and it is said one clap is for O'Sensei if there is a picture of him present and one clap is for god.

Above: The seated bow.

How to practice properly

In the practice hall, work with your opponent should be firm, but always with an eye toward cooperation. This does not mean that you fall down for your opponent, but rather that you work with him or her to provide exactly the kind of practice they require. This is an especially important thing if you are a teacher. Knowing your student's limitations and needs will allow you to structure the practice to their maximum benefit.

Left: The standing bow properly executed.

All students in a club should back each other up. If one man is not doing well, the others should do what they can to help. Most practice halls are incubators for improved individuals – but that improvement happens quicker and more effectively when everyone is working together.

Necessary exercises

In order to be able to practice properly, it is important that warm-up and exercise regimens specifically designed for martial arts like Aikido be employed. Some of these important exercises have gone missing from many clubs because they are difficult and painful. However, the little pain experienced while conducting the exercises will save you from a whole lot of pain later. Warm-up should include, but is not limited to: Puss-ups on the backs of the wrists, sit-ups, leg stretches, taisabaki and irimi exercises, extension exersises, wrist, elbow and shoulder stretches, leg stretches, limbering of the back and neck and ukime exercises.

How to conduct yourself with your opponent

Your opponent deserves unswerving respect. If he is your practice partner, you should want him to continue to practice enthusiastically with you, and subsequently, respect is very important. If your opponent is a real attacker, you want to dispatch him with dignity, honor and precision so that when the contest is finished it can be said that you conducted yourself appropriately. Additionally, should you lose in this real-world fight, at least you presented a proper accounting of yourself and can leave the world honorably.

How to treat weapons

Weapons should always be treated the same – regardless of whether they are a simple stick, a longsword or a gun. Each weapon brings with it its own set of dangers. Without respect and discipline, someone will likely get hurt. When taking a weapon which is offered to you by someone, you should remember to bow. This is done in different ways according to the weapon and the situation in which it is being given to you, but it is done for your opponent and the weapon itself. Generally speaking, the weapon is taken with your left hand, you bow by placing your forehead to the weapon, and it is then placed at your left side. A bow to your opponent follows.

Proper behavior with visitors

Visitors to the club are either prospective students, or teachers, students from another class. Often they are feeling a bit out of place and have come to either learn more technique, experience practice with a new group of people, or just meet people with the same interests they have. Many times I have practiced at clubs in various places I have visited – and although they were martial artists of different styles, I found the atmosphere to be warm and familiar. Often visitors just want a brief respite in a familiar place when they're out travelling.

Subsequently, as fellow students, you should welcome them and make them feel like the lost sisters and brothers they are. As teachers, you should make your visitor feel comfortable and allow them the luxury of practicing technique with your group.

> Combat is like a musical score. Like music there are spaces in between. These spaces are where the true aspects of combat exist.

Dealing with resistance

Resistance or defensive actions during a technique is a reasonable thing. Without it, we would be doing something akin to ballroom dancing. Resistance should be welcomed on the mat. However, too much resistance, or resistance at the wrong time can be dangerous.

Aikido practitioners – indeed any martial art practitioner – needs to remember always that the techniques they are practicing and developing were once meant for the battlefield, and as such, can be devastating if care is not exercised in their employment.

The attacker on the mat also needs to be aware that their resistance is useful up until the moment the technique goes on. To resist beyond that is courting disaster. You may get away with it 99 times, but that 100th technique is going to make up for all the times you escaped.

However, it's always important to note that removal of all resistance in the name of safety is perhaps even more dangerous. If a student believes they can defend themselves, but never practices with resistance, they will at some point be attempting to make a technique which will not work. If that occurs during an actual attack, the situation could end poorly.

A good rule of thumb is this: When practicing with a slightly lower grade, or an equal, conduct your technique the way you would like it applied to you. If you are both strong men, feel free to practice with greater spirit. If not, then practice at a reduced level. If your opponent is a much lower grade, you must practice with gentleness and compassion. If they are more senior to you, however, attack strongly and make some reasonable resistance.

Honoring your school

It is one thing to come to practice every time and practice and then go home. This is a person who means very little to a club. On the other hand, the student who comes to practice with enthusiasm, always with ideas to better things for the clubs; who is not afraid of taking responsibility for a project; who assists in keeping the dojo in order and who is always there for sensei and his fellow students – this person is worth much. By doing these things, he or she brings honor and respect into a club. This kind of person is very important to the teacher because they show that the lessons being learned in the dojo are valuable ones and prove over and over again that it's important to continue to pass on the training.

Showing respect to your teacher

A good teacher has literally spent their lives developing the technique you see them perfrom during demonstrations or in class. At this stage, they are not interested in developing themselves, but have begun to put everything they have into developing you. A traditional teacher would ask little in return – help with the rent of the dojo, or with the upkeep of the place – some would just ask that you show up

Senior student's checklist

Training hard, not stupid

There's a fine line between training hard and going to far. Hard training should always raise the level of the technique being performed – stupid training will cause it to stagnate or decay. One important rule is to remain traditional to the degree that you're passing on technique as it was first shown to you. Leave out the refinements and practice the bare bones. The practices should be vigorous at the end of which you feel drained, but happy you came.

A stupid practice will result in a lot of bangs, bruises, loosened teeth and sore or pulled muscles with people unable to get on the mat again for a period of time. This is precisely the kind of thing you don't want.

Senior grades should be pressured and they should be pushed to exceed the limitations they've placed on themselves, but if that means producing injuries, then it's time to tone things down.

A good practice can take things right to the edge of sanity, allowing people to gain tremendous improvements and insight.

Keeping control of the dojo

Tradition and etiquette should be maintained always. Where it slips is a potential for injury – either at that moment, or later in that student's life. As a senior grade, your actions must be without question. You must do your best to uphold the traditions of the club and embody its ideals. Remember, regardless of whether you've attended class for ten days or ten years, you are a representative of that club, your martial art, your teacher and his teachers. You must also hold the other members of the club to this standard as well – and remind them firmly of it if need be.

Choosing when to lose

As a student moves up the ranks he is always interested in making his technique more effective – at least in our school. This can cause problems as he is working hard to become unstoppable – a goal which can be achieved in fairly short order, but which will be accompanied usually by an impressive lack of grace.

So, although the mid-grade student now has the capacity to make technique in most cases, he or she doesn't know when to quit. A senior student's responsibility is to develop this capacity for some degree of compassion, while still maintaining their level as a powerful technician.

I call this "choosing when to lose," and it's applicable to more than just the martial art. The senior student should look toward the time when they too may become teachers, and they should realize that the development of the new student is just as important as their own development. In fact, the two are tied together.

In my opinion, the best kind of club is the one where senior students assist the junior grades in learning technique – great insights come from this for both parties.

Identifying a beginner's motivation

A beginner often doesn't really know why they have come to practice. When I was grading up, there were days I would very seriously ask myself that question, "why am I here." By the time I left my teachers for the United States in 1990, I still didn't know what had brought me to practice in that place. Of course, by then it didn't matter – I was on my way to becoming something different. Now that I think back on it, however, I think it must have been a fantastic sense of the individual that allowed my teachers to help motivate me to keep practicing. So, today I do the same with my students. It is important to discover the thing that keeps them coming back to practice – that's the carrot – and it's also important to use hard training and discipline to keep them interested – that's the stick.

Working with other martial artists

The senior student may find himself visiting other clubs, or talking and practicing with other martial artists of varying disciplines. This contact should not be used as some type of contest. Remember that although you may beat your opponent, it really means nothing. It's just two dogs fighting and whichever one's teeth are the sharpest that day – he will win. In the end you accomplish nothing by doing this. However, if you enter this meeting with an open mind and work toward the exchange of ideas and training, then you will have accomplished something very important. You will have a new friend or friends and you will open doors that would otherwise have remained shut to meeker members of your club. It's always true – any training at all will broaden your experience and teach you new things.

Asking questions

The senior student or teacher often gets lost in the minutia of technique and forgets that there are questions he or she can ask. The day those questions don't come is the day you are no longer developing. Ask questions and always work to provide answers.

Tolerance

Remember this always: Not everyone was born with all the faculties and abilities you may believe you have been graced with. Sometimes, you may be faced with an individual who just has a need to feel better about himself, to belong to something, or to provide something to others. These people require tolerance, compassion and understanding and should be treated as you would treat anyone else in the club.

Why does the Ellis School use colored belts

At the Ellis School we also use colored belts as Judoka do, to represent the kyu grades of the pupil.

In a very large club with one class for each kyu grade, there is no problem. But very few club dojos are large enough in number of pupils to allow this.

It is much safer in mixed kyu groups to have instant recognition of a pupils kyu grade. A higher grade can apply technique which would harm a lower grade (who may not be able to ukemi or escape or submit without injury).

Also, for a visiting teacher, it is easy to pull an unknown student from a group to demonstrate a technique at that level.

-Eastman

Troubleshooting Technique

Often, people have very simple difficulties with techniques – and many times these are the same difficulties as other people have. Following is a list of common mistakes and some photos to show what is being done wrong and what to do to correct it.

Wrong   **Right**

Distance in Shihonage
Shihonage requires a strong entry into the technique and absolute precision when you're stepping in. Depending on the version of this technique which is being used, your feet may end up in different locations respective to your opponent. However, the body always remains tight to your opponent, so that even a single sheet of paper could not be placed between you.

Poor projection in Shihonage
Shihonage requires prior to the throw, that the weight of the body be shifted through the hips to take your opponent. With improper projection and poor timing, the technique can go flat.

Wrong   **Right**

Not looking your direction in kotegaeshe
A person effecting kotegaeshe must keep their head in line with the rest of their body and look the direction they are turning. Without this, they can be struck in the face, or will be unable to get good extension in their technique. Worse, they will not know what is waiting for them on their blind side, if they don't turn and look.

Poor lead in kotegaeshe
Leading is important throughout kotegaeshe. As you make your turn to avoid or escape the attack, you must continue the direction of your opponent by projecting his hand and wrist outward. Often, students will simply tug on the arm, or pull their opponent around. This is not right. For the technique to work properly, extension must be applied through the technique, making it a "leading" motion as opposed to a push or pull.

Keeping on center in kotegaeshe
The opponent's job is not to cooperate with you, but to attack and defend himself. If you do not keep his wrist at your centerline after the lead, you will give him back his balance and strength and he will have succeeded.

Wrong

Not turning hips enough in kotegaeshe
Without a proper hip turn, this technique loses much of its power and most of its effectiveness. A hip turn is accomplished when the opponent's wrist is held securely at your waist or is thrust back into their face – in either case – while on centerline. The turn must be sharp, placing the force and weight of your body on their trapped arm (wrist). What is often done by the new practitioner is to use the upper body strength to muscle the technique onto the wrist.

Not entering shoulder-to-shoulder in iriminage
If your entry into iriminage is improper, you will be unable to effectively lead your opponent and a gap will widen between the two of you, making it impossible to finish the technique safely or effectively. This problem can be partially avoided by entering strongly so that your shoulder touches theirs. The rest of the technique then follows.

Not keeping the head on the shoulder in iriminage
This problem will also lead to a widening gap between you and your opponent. The head must remain pinned to your shoulder, or the technique will flatten out and your opponent will spin away from you as you turn. To prevent this, hold your outside hand firmly to press your opponent's head onto your shoulder.

Right

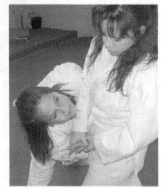

Not stepping 180 degrees in iriminage

If as you enter the lead, you only step backwards at 45 degrees (or any less than 180), your opponent will not be properly off-balance and you will fail. To prevent this, concentrate on stepping straight backwards once you've taken your opponent's skull onto your shoulder. The tendency is to make the negative step backwards too oblique. This will cause serious problems in the final moments of the movement.

Not turning the hips in iriminage

Hips being the center of all technique are no less important in iriminage. As the final moment of the technique approaches, the hips should be turning to face the direction you are throwing your opponent. If this does not happen, the power in the technique will be greatly reduced.

Not extending arm properly at technique end.

The arm nearest your opponent, which moves up his bodyline and extends past his head, should be stretched out with thumb facing down and palm outwards at the technique's end. Any other position allows your opponent greater options once he hits the ground.

Not leading in tenchinage

Although tenchinage appears to be a simple task of walking through the opponent, there are actually a number of principles at work here. The arm which is cutting down the attack (or leading into it), must extend downward; in effect, leading your opponent to turn and face the opposite direction or become unbalanced. Without this good entry and lead, the opponent's balance will not be split, and the technique will go flat.

Wrong

Right

Wrong

Right

Kotegaeshe problem solving.

Right

Wrong

Tenchinage problem solving.

Not extending in tenchinage

If your opponent is not becoming unbalanced in tenchinage, there may be two reasons. First, as described previously, a good lead is necessary. But also important is proper extension. Without extension (stepping forward through your opponent and bringing the outside arm up through the bodyline), the technique will not work, and your opponent may only stagger backward a couple of steps.

Not using hips in tenchinage

If as you enter for the throw, you are not following through with the hips, tenchinage will very likely fail. It's important to remember for this technique, that the body moves all together, as a unit.

Not enough spirit in tenchinage

Tenchinage is all about intent. If you are unable to focus, the technique will also fail. Good timing, overwhelming positive movement, lead and extend, and unswerving intention will carry you through. If any of these factors are lacking, the technique will be ineffective.

Not stepping in a zig-zag for tenchinage

This mode of stepping with tenchinage is primarily focused at beginners. It's important to realize that while your hands are making distinctive motions, so are your feet. In this case, you should be stepping outward (at an angle) with your outside foot and inward (at an angle) with your inside foot. Practicing this motion will build good form for tenchhinage.

Not leading all the way to the floor with kaitenage

Kaitenage must be accomplished with more than 55 percent of your opponent's balance and weight shifted forward. They must be doubled-over in order for this to be effective. The opponent can be bent with an atemi to the stomach, and a follow-up attack to the groin. If your movement is fluid, you can then carry their hands to the floor and upward behind their back in an arc.

Not keeping arms in proper locations for kaitenage

For kaitenage (indeed, it could be argued, for all technique) the arms should remain in-line with the body. To turn them so that the elbows are away from the body, or to turn the arms off center will cause the technique to produce unpredictable results.

Not keeping palms up through the kaitenage throw

The palms must always remain facing upward, as this is the traditional technique. Kaitenage can be applied, however, with the hands in alternative positions, although this tends to alter the dynamics of the technique.

Not turning hips enough in kaitenage throw

You can't make a throw in kaitenage unless you turn the hips. They should squarely face the direction you are throwing your opponent.

Not brushing the back of the opponent's head with arm in kaitenage

As you turn your hips to make the throw in kaitenage, your inside arm should brush the back of your opponent's head and neck. If this is not done, the technique is not proper, and it may result in a poor throw, or no throw at all.

Not stepping through in kaitenage

If this technique is done without stepping through at the end as you take the throw, much of the force is reduced and your own balance may suffer. As the arms sweep across the back of the head and your hips turn to face the direction of the throw, simply try stepping forward.

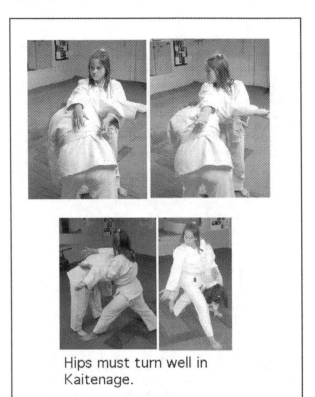

Hips must turn well in Kaitenage.

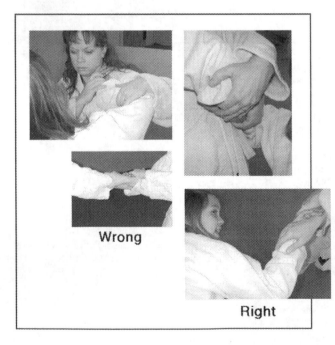

Wrong

Right

Not properly turning from the hips for nikkyo

Nikkyo will lose most of its power when you incorrectly turn your wrist over your opponent's and when you refuse to turn your hips into the technique. The hips must turn to increase the power in the movement.

Not extending the fingers for nikkyo

Nikkyo must be executed with the fingers of the hand extended, and they must turn through an arc back toward your own belly. If this is not done, the technique will be ineffective.

The opponent's arm must remain parallel to the floor

During the application of the wrist turn in nikkyo, the opponent's elbow must not drop below his hand; or rise above it. The opponent's arm must remain level with the floor thorughout the application of the technique. If this does not happen, and the elbow is allowed to rise, the opponent can turn away from you allowing him to kick and forcing you into a desperate attempt to take ikkyo instead. If the elbow drops, the opponent can then easily strike you with the hand.

Grabbing the wrist in nikkyo

All the fingers should remain on top of the opponent's wrist in nikkyo, including the thumb. To place the thumb under the wrist will restrict the application of the technique.

Using too much strength in nikkyo

Nikkyo doesn't require strength. If you are struggling with the technique you are not turning the wrist properly, not controlling the level of the opponent's arm, etc.

Not extending enough in ikkyo

The opponent's arm must be firmly extended at the elbow when taking ikkyo. If extension is poor, the opponent will not move – they will simply remain where they are, thier balance unaffected. Concentrate on pushing the elbow in an arc toward the opponent's ear. The wrist should be directed in a sweeping downward motion as the body turns with both arms remaining in line.

Not taking the elbow in a downward crescent for ikkyo
The elbow must follow the wrist in that extreme downward crescent for the technique to be effective.

Not touching the floor before taking control of wrist for sankkyo
You must move through the lead as if you were going to touch the floor as you take the wrist for sankkyo. Without this, the opponent is not unbalanced, and the traditional version of the technique can not be accomplished properly.

Not keeping a square with the opponent's arm in sankkyo
People tend to lose control of sankkyo, or find it ineffective because they have not maintained a square with the arm they are grasping. This square must be maintained through to the throw.

Wrong

Right

Right

Not turning the wrist properly in sankkyo application
If the wrist is not turned properly in application of the throw or to take control techniques, sankkyo will go flat. The turn should feel like a wave-like motion. In the throw, the heel of the hand should be facing the direction you are throwing your opponent.

Not keeping the arm in centerline of body against chest
For sankkyo to be effective, complete control must be maintained of the vertical forearm of your opponent. This entails keeping the arm braced against your chest. If it comes away, the technique can still be applied relatively effectively, but it requires more energy to do it.

Not moving from the hips in application of the throw
With sankkyo, the hips must shift forward for the throw. If this does not happen, the tendency is for the opponent to stagger forward and stop short of being thrown.

The erosion of Aikido

Whilst there are still a few good dojos in the UK teaching traditional Aikido, I feel that many abuse the word "traditional" and a lot of the Aikido bears very little resemblance to the early Aikido that I studied in the 1950s.

In those early days, Kenshiro Abbe Sensei and Ken Williams Sensei both taught hard Aikido, often using a shinai to get a particular point across. Both Derek Eastman Sensei and I still on occasion use this method when necessary. In those early days, every student of Aikido would do press-ups on the backs of their wrists, some with the hands turned inwards and some with the hands turned outwards; this is a very hard exercise. It not only makes the wrists strong, but supple. It would now appear that we in the Ellis Schools are the only ones still doing these exercises.

Teachers and students of Aikido often refer to "Ki" as if it were some form of mysterious magic. I believe that "Ki" is developed through hard training and building your strength of spirit.

I still teach the old "Traditional" style of Aikido, and have very little time for the fantasy style of "dancing aikido" which can only be practiced by two students who know each other's movement. As a form of self defence, it would only work if one was attacked by another student from the same dojo.

Most genuine students who know of the true origins of Aikido in the UK, also respect the teachers of that time for the effort they put into the promotion of Aikido.

When I read the "history" of many Aikido teachers, you would never know that they were taught by Ken Williams sensei and the other instructors from the Hut. It would appear they are going through some kind of credibility crisis. The several years spent with an English teacher have no bearing on their Aikido career, so this is conveniently omitted and these lost years are covered by a few weekends with a Japanese teacher. Then we read, "Oh yes, I was trained by Chiba Sensei, etc. etc."

I have often heard of teachers who say that they trained at the Hut in the early days. Only recently, a visiting student said to me, "Sensei, do you remember my teacher? He trained at the Hut in the early days."

"I'm sorry," I said. "But I was at the Hut for 20 years and I have never heard of your teacher."

On Atemi

It would now appear that most Aikidoists no longer approve of atemi in practice. If we look at O'Sensei in his prime (45 to 55-years-old), we see something interesting. Take for example his book, "Budo" where he shows a series of techniques – in every one of these, he makes atemi at some point.

Abbe Sensei paid great emphasis to punching and kicking as part of our general exercise and training, with at least 30 minutes of punching and kicking every session. The attack would always be on target, and if your face was still there and you got hit, sensei would say that it was your own fault for not moving out of the way.

Abbe Sensei was a very positive man in whatever martial art he was demonstrating. At one venue in Acton London, he was demonstrating sword kata with Tomio O'Tani, the British National Coach for Kendo.

As Tomio attacked with shomen, Abbe sensei then made the fastest irimi I have ever seen.

Tomio had thick, black hair in a fringe, hanging over his forehead. In what appeared to be a flash of steel – and as the whole audience made gasping noises of shock – we thought the attack was turning into a tragedy. Tomio never moved, and those in the front row said he never even blinked, but the sword was touching his forehead, and although there was no blood, on the floor was the fringe part of Tomio's hair.

Tomio was a great friend of mine, and after the demonstration was over I asked how he felt about what had happened.

"Abbe Sensei never did like my fringe," he said.

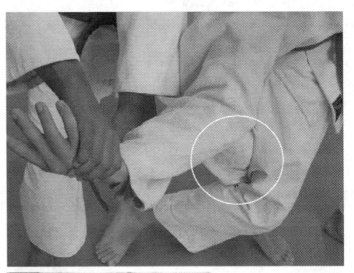

On the next few pages are demonstrated various types of atemi which can be used inside the standard techniques practiced in Aikido. It should be noted that the atemi used should produce a complimentary effect, allowing you to better complete the desired defense. This technique (Shihonage), is augmented by a solid kick to the opponent's leg before entering.

Atemi

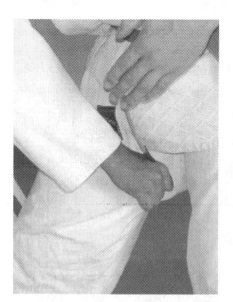

In iriminage, the atemi can be applied upon entering the technique. Here you can see the strike to the groin prior to taking the opponent off-balance.

Atemi within the technique kotegaeshe

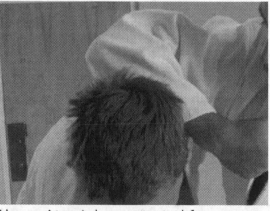

Atemi as it is applied within the technique kotegeashe can be accomplished with the elbow as pressure is going on the wrist.

Left: A kick to help get your opponent to the ground can be accomplished during nikkyo. Below: An elbow strike entering sankkyo.

Left: Following the elbow strike, a follow-up to the groin.

Above: Atemi demonstrated from tenchinage. Left, a knee or kick delivered while entering into ikkyo. Below: The same strike with sankkyo.

Left : A pin from iriminage. This is commonly used when disarming an opponent.

Pins and holds

Another item which can be applied to the techniques is the pin. There are dozens of different pins which can be used in conjunction with the traditional versions of the Aikido techniques. Following are a fe of these:

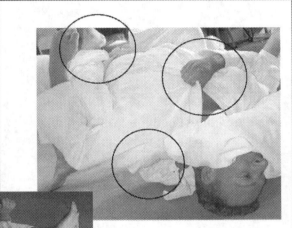

An uncomfortable pin which can be applied to arch the opponent's neck and back. Note the three points of control.

Left and below:
A pin from the mount position as it can be applied to shihonage.

Right: Two possible pins which can be achieved after moving through kotegaeshe.

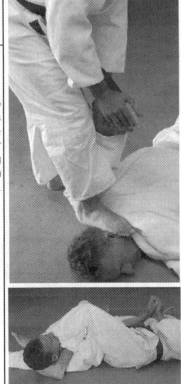

Here is a pin taken from an oblique attack with a club. It is possible to see here that the immobilization occurs before the technique hits the ground.

Here are two possible pins which can be taken directly following tenchinage.

Left and below: two possible pins from ikkyo.

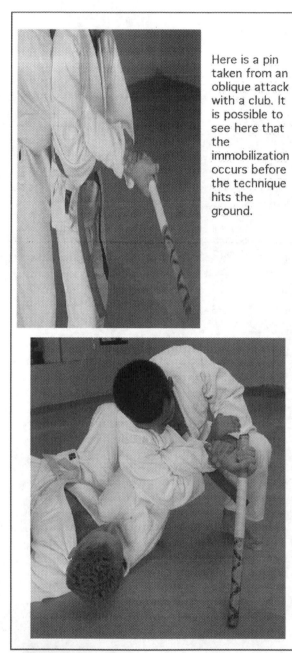

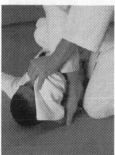

Left: Shihonage can be easily taken to a pin. Pictured here is a pin which keeps the attacking arm immobilized while allowing a strike after the lower hand releases its grip.

Below: Al Montemar of the Ellis
School's Texas Club, demonstrates
knife technique with Dave Rogers at
Blackdam in 1989.

Weapons Technique

Jo kata

On the following pages is the entire two-man jo kata currently being
practiced and taught by the Ellis Schools.

Demonstrated by Sensei Derek
Eastman and Sensei Mark Eastman

The first 28 movements of this kata can also be performed and practiced as a single-man kata. The grip is a bojutsu fighting posture and not the similar spear posture. These are distinguished by having the palms of the hands facing the same direction while holding the staff - not alternating.

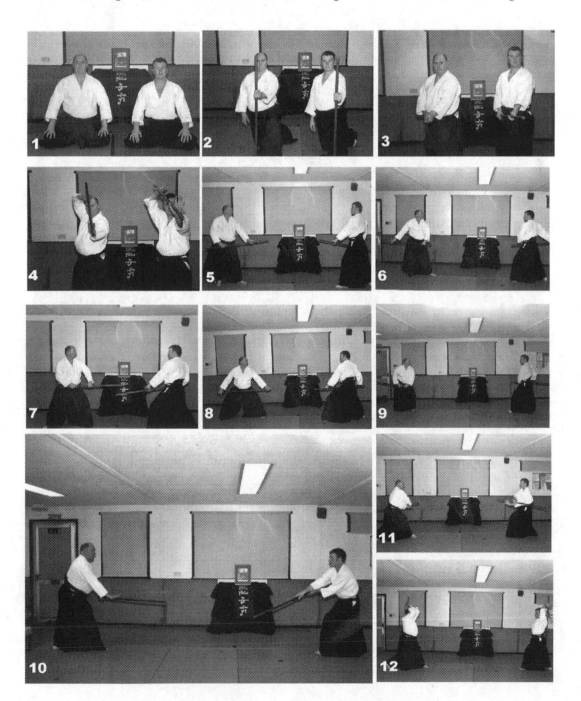

A notable movement in this kata is the rolling defense pictured in frame 19. This defense utilizes the rearward rolling movement of the jo to deflect an advancing weapon. A subsequent reversal of this movement can return your weapon to an active attack much quicker than your opponent can recover.

Throughout this kata, movement incorporates irimi, taisabaki and atemi. Below you can see how the weapon is used to defend against attack - usually at an angle, ensuring that the direct force of the opponent's weapon is not absorbed by the jo.

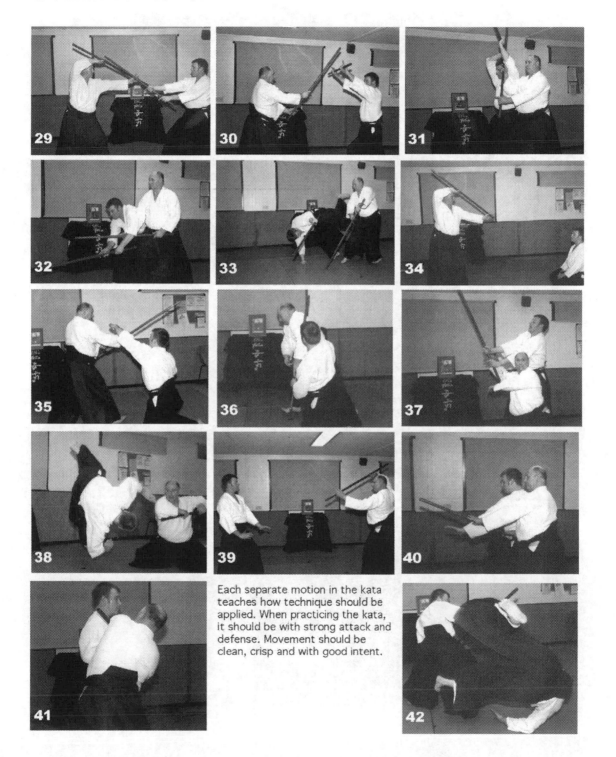

Each separate motion in the kata teaches how technique should be applied. When practicing the kata, it should be with strong attack and defense. Movement should be clean, crisp and with good intent.

Note the use of atemi (below) to take the balance and position of your opponent. The weapon always follows through and it's the opponent's responsibility to avoid getting hit.

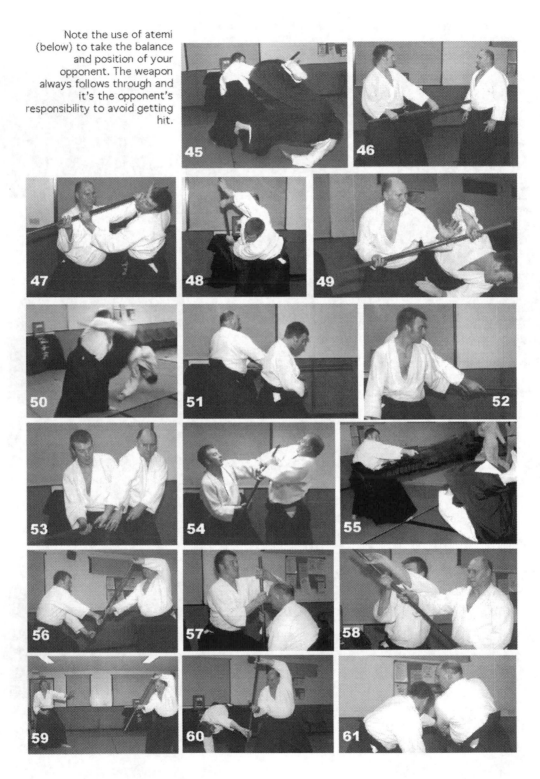

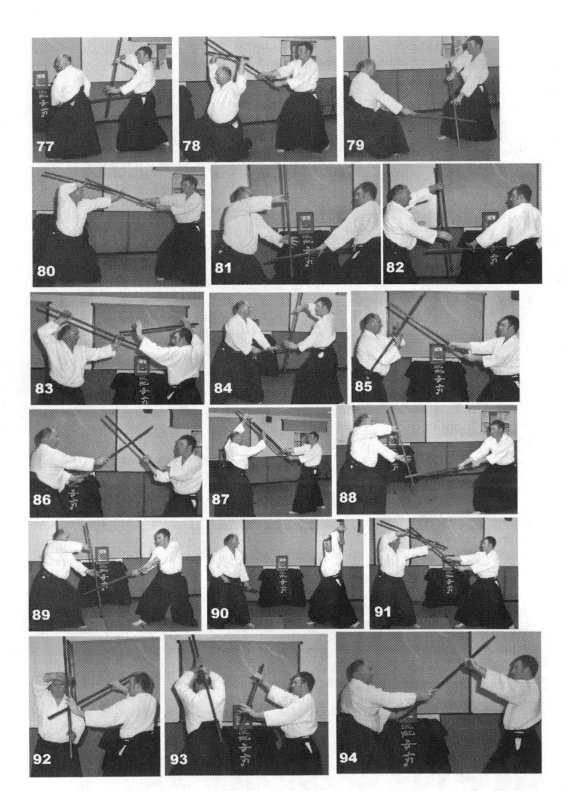

Above, the final two defense movements in the jo kata.

Left and below is pictured one empty-hand defense against attack with a jo. To make this effective, it is necessary to move into the opponent immediately. The closer you can get to the attacker, the less force the attack will have had time to generate.

Below, the opponent is taken all the way to the mat and pressure is applied to the elbow to control the weapon.

It's important with weapons to practice their use as well as the appropriate defenses against their use. Following are some examples of defense against an opponent using a short staff.

Defense against attack with a jo

Here is a simple empty-hand defense against an attack by an opponent weilding a jo.

Here are two additional defenses against an opponent attacking with a jo. The most important thing to remember with these is that you

must enter as your opponent's weapon is moving forward to strike. If you don't stay close to your opponent; or if you don't enter deep enough, these techniques will be impossible.

Another alternative ending to the technique pictured on the page opposite this one.

Good extension is necessary to dislodge your opponent.

Weapons Technique

Sword

.

Sword technique for Aikido

Many Aikido schools today either discount the sword in practicing Aikido technique, or use it as though it were some kind of baton.

In fact, proper grip and use of the sword is very important to developing effective Aikido technique. To practice Aikido without practicing cutting with the sword leaves an entire level of the technique unexplored.

Here in this small section you will see examples of proper posture (above left), and some exercises with bokken.

The first exercise for sword is the standard suburi cut. This is accomplished as depicted at left. With these practice cuts, the bokken is brought all the way back, stretching out the arms and opening the chest. For development of wrists, arms and shoulders, 250 - 500 cuts a day with suburito is considered to be reasonable.

Men: A cut to center of head.

Yokomen: A cut to the side of the head.

Kote: A cut to the wrist.

Right: The proper grip for the sword turns both hands inward so that pressure from the cut is not delivered through the back of the hand, but is rather absorbed up through the arms and into the body.

Do: A cut to center.

Above is a series of simple exercises utilizing the strike points from Kendo. This exercise develops control in the cut and improves and defines an Aikido student's posture and balance while moving.

Defense against knife

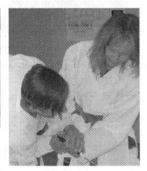

Following are some defenses used against knife. This technique is actually the same as is seen in 6th Form previously in this book. With or without a weapon, the technique doesn't change much. In the case of the movement below, the single change is the location of the weapon and the opponent's hand as the technique is applied. In this case, the weapon is thrust back towards the opponent's throat.

It's important to take this technique firmly. Losing your grip on the opponent's wrist once you've entered the technique would be disasterous. Demonstrated here is kotegaeshe.

Sankyo against knife attack.

These defenses against knife are very dangerous and should be practiced with great caution. Pictured here is shihonage against knife.

Here is tenchinage against knife with a follow-through lock against the arm.

Ikkyo against knife attack.

There is no emotion in the mirror of combat
unless we reflect it there ourselves.

ELEMENTS OF TRADITION

Histories

The following section contains a brief history of the beginning of
Aikido in Britain and the founding and continuance of The Ellis
Schools of Traditional Aikido in the United Kingdom and the United
States.

The contents of this section includes:

A beginning

The early years

Nakazono Sensei

The Salesmen

Mad Geoff

Right: Kenshiro Abbe Sensei watches as Henry Ellis performs technique in the Hut, 1960. Below: Abbe issuing some clear instruction.

Above: The Abbe School of Budo in the late 1950s. Pictured center, front is Kenshiro Abbe, one of Morihei Ueshiba's students and the man who brought Aikido to Britain in 1955. Pictured in the back row, second man from the right, is Henry Ellis, who today is one of only four teachers left in the world from the Abbe School of Budo.

A beginning

Tired from travelling and looking forward to more difficult work ahead, the young man looked for a seat on the crowded train.

Settling next to a stocky, old man, he sat back against the swaying side of the car.

"Don't I know you," said the old man next to him.

Sighing the young man looked over into the wrinkling face beside him. "I don't think so."

"Yes I'm sure I know you," said the old man, "what is your name?"

The young man sat up, facing his new companion more directly. Looking fiercely at the old man, he announced proudly, "I am Kenshiro Abbe, champion of all Japan."

The old man smiled, "Ahh, yes, I knew I had seen you before."

"Please could you be quiet now," asked Abbe, settling back in his seat. "I have a competition I am going to and I need to get some rest."

"Of course," said the old man.

As the train ground along the winding track, however, the old man didn't stop talking. He continued to drone on incessantly, till finally Abbe sat up and again faced him.

"Be quiet, old man!" he said, " I need to sleep!"

"If I am just an old man, and you are such a great Judo champion, then perhaps you can break my finger. I will be quiet if you can break my little finger," said the old man.

Thinking that he may finally be rid of the old man, the young man scrutinized the single digit that was held out to him. Tired and a little angry, he grabbed the finger and twisted to break it. What followed, however, wasn't the dry, small snapping sound he'd expected. Instead, he was airborne – slamming down onto the floor of the train; all the air whuffing out of him. Worse still, he was immobilized. After a moment, the old man let him up.

"Who are you?" asked Abbe in wonderment.

"I am Moreihei Ueyshiba, founder of Aikido," said the man.

Abbe, still on the floor of the car, bowed to the old man and asked if he could come to his dojo to train. He was accepted as a student and would stay with Ueyshiba for ten years.

More than forty years later another young man walked the corridors of a sports center in Britain. He and his friend had come to watch a Tai Chi demonstration, but finding the teacher to have questionable qualifications, left the room and was now looking for the exit.

As Americans , the two young men were in Britain as part of the ground-launched cruise missile system. They were U.S. Air Force members stationed at the newly reopened Greenham Common Air Base – just a half-hour from the Basingstoke Sports Center, which they were now lost in.

Walking down a dark corridor, they passed through another set of double doors – and inadvertently walked into another martial art class.

Fascinated, the two men sat in some plastic chairs which

were thrust up against the wall.

"What is this?" whispered the smaller one.

The big one, of Phillipino descent, had practiced Judo for a long time, and was better schooled in the martial arts. Squinting out at the children who were practicing on the mat, he leaned over to his companion.

"I'm not sure, but I think this is Aikido," he said.

At these words, the doors again swung open and a tall, grey-haired gentleman came into the room, standing next to the two younger men. Not saying a word, the old man just stared out at the group for a moment, then someone noticed him and the whole class stopped and bowed in his direction.

He returned the bow as the doors opened again.

This time, a long line of men came in, taking up their positions on the opposite side of the mat. What followed would mark the beginning of a new course in the lives of the two young American visitors. They would return again the following week and continue to return – until years later, Greenham Common was closed down and they were sent back to the States.

Still, they had practiced with legends – Derek Eastman Sensei and Henry Ellis Sensei; two of the last remaining students of Kenshiro Abbe, the legendary Judo Champion and master of several other martial arts, including the earliest form of traditional Aikido.

In the days when Eastman and Ellis had first walked onto the mat, training was done at a place called "The Hut."

The young man winced as he used the outdoor spigot to wash his feet. It was fall in Britain and there were few places in the world which made outdoor bathing – even just partial outdoor bathing – so miserable.

It might be bloody freezing in Alaska, the young man thought, but the wet British climate made for a different kind of cold. It was a cold which climbed up into you and sat at the pit of your stomach – the kind of chill that didn't slap into you, but rather slowly pushed at you until later in life, your bones ached and your breath caught in your throat as your feet kissed the wood of the bedroom floor in the early morning.

But this was nothing to be concerned about now. The old man had told him to go wash his feet – and no one argued with the old man.

As the water screemed over his feet, the young man tried hard to think about something else. Choking back what could have been a girlish yelp had it escaped his lips, he gazed at the

building beyond the spigot.

It was the back of an old English pub that he stared at. Timber-framed, the place was clothed in long wooden slats layed in horizontally. Its double back doors with their long iron hinges were painted over in some kind of cheap, dark red oil based paint which seemed to be perpetually chipping and peeling. This was Southern Britain and the building was a fairly common one for the Hillingdon area. Here at the back door to the pub, there was a long, thin concrete walkway nearly lost in the encroaching grass and two tall concrete steps.

Today, the crushed brown leaves of fall had collected against these steps and in the process of crunching through them on the way to the pub, the young man had carried some of the bits and pieces into the room beyond that door. Subsequently he was back outside again freezing his ass off. But better that, than piss off the old man.

Trying hard not to get his feet dirty again (which was difficult, because now they were completely numb), the man stumbled across the grass and back through the tall red doors. Inside, the atmosphere was tense. Then again - when wasn't it tense in here?

Gathered around the edges of a large canvas mat were a couple dozen people clothed in the traditional white uniform of those practicing the traditional fighting styles of the Japanese. This back room of the pub called "The Hut," had been rented some time ago to a somewhat senior Japanese man, Kenshiro Abbe, (8th Dan Judo, 6th Dan Kyudo, 6th Dan Kendo, 6th Dan Karate and 6th Dan Aikido) for the instruction of Judo and Karate. The local response to this had been good, and students had come from all over to learn the "secrets" the old man was willing to impart.

The club at this time in 1955 was comprised of nearly 35 regular students. Among these were men who would many years later make their names in the world of Aikido; Ken Williams, Haydyn Foster, Lennie Ballard, Eric Dollimore and Henry "Harry" Ellis.

Today, the "Abbe School of Budo," which had flourished in the 50s and 60s with the spread of Asian fighting systems to the West, has long since closed its doors. But the grand old building, "The Hut," continues as a martial art training center under the direction of one of its early students - now a revered teacher, himself - Sensei Hadyn Foster.

Still, in the early 1950s, when Aikido was a guarded secret in Japan, only Judo and Karate were being taught at The Hut. In 1955, as students got on the mat for a practice, at Kenshiro Abbe's second dojo in King's Cross, East London all that changed.

Henry Ellis (on the bunk in the background) watches as two fellow teachers (Tomio Otani and Tom Weir) play the guitar late one evening during one of the first Aikido summer school sessions in Britain around 1960.

"It was there that Kenshiro Abbe introduced Aikido," said Henry Ellis, today a 5th Dan of Aikido with more than 45 years experience. "Sensei Abbe said he'd received this letter from Japan and was then able to teach to any student who wanted to study Aikido. Mr. Williams was his first student, who then took a handful of us and began bringing them up to Dan Grade under the direct instruction of Kenshiro Abbe."

Training under these conditions was brutal. Students were running nearly 13 miles, three days a week, before practice, and any corrections on the mat were handled with very little spoken words – usually just a slap with a shinai (bamboo sword).

"Mr. Williams always followed the way Abbe Sensei taught, and that was to hit with a shinai when something was wrong," said Ellis. "The theory, of course, was that while Abbe Sensei could not speak very good English, the shinai spoke fluently."

This painful method of learning had a deeper meaning, though. Because although you can tell a person twenty times what to do and they will forget twenty times, you can tell them once with a shinai and they'll never forget.

The shinai, as it turns out had a lot of interesting uses.

On the mat, poor technique in punching exercises would result in a rack of shinais being strapped to your back ensuring that the strikes had to come from the hip; and that the shoulders would not be thrown forward.

Williams, the first student of Aikido in Britain, appeared to be a small-framed, almost delicate individual, but in those early days, he was a powerful practitioner of traditional Aikido, and those students he had were brought up in a fairly unforgiving atmosphere, with the constant oversight of Abbe Sensei.

Gradings were difficult, and in this period, were always administered by Abbe.

The very first Aikido seminar held in Britain encompassed only three students of the art – Hadyn Foster, Eric Dolleymore and Henry Ellis.

"The first summer school had three students, and the hardest thing to bear was that this was our vacation," said Ellis. "And of course Abbe Sensei's main committment on this course was to Judo; Yukio Otani, an elderly Judo master was there with Tommy Otani, his son and the national coach for Kendo. So with all these things going on, there was really no one to give a damn about three or four students of Aikido. So, we went into the fields surrounding the sports center and practiced there during the day.

Professor Henry Ellis stands at the door to The Hut where he was a student of Ken Williams and Kenshiro Abbe many years ago.

We were only allowed to use the mats at night when the other students had finished. That was the first seminar. But within a year, at the following summer school, Aikido became one of the major players."

At this time in the late 50s, a new student began training under Ken Williams and Kenshiro Abbe. As Ellis had made his dan grade, it was suggested that he should choose an assistant from amongst some of the higher grade students. When he told Abbe that he wanted this new student instead, Abbe objected. But Ellis stood his ground, and this is how he became associated with Derek Eastman, who today as a 5th dan and one of the most respected teachers of Aikido in Britain, still remains a loyal assistant to Ellis. In the early days, however, the two trained continuously at The Hut, and at some of the other associated dojos around London.

"Mr. Eastman and I used to study with Tommy Otani, who was close in age to us and a good friend," said Ellis. "Because the movements of Kendo are very similar to Aikido, we used to go to his club in Acton and study there. In fact, the only thing I carried on with after beginning to study Aikido was Kendo. I wanted to learn more sword technique and I enjoyed the exercise. Mr. Eastman and I used to smash the hell out of each other in each session."

Back at the Hut, practices were still moving hard, fast and direct.

Abbe's Aikido was a version taught to him by Ueyshiba prior to WWII. The techniques incorporated no-nonsense straight lines emphasizing powerful entries and almost always including the use of atemi. The first of the new teachers of Aikido to arrive in Britain was Matsuharu Nakazono, a younger man sent to teach the more modern version of Aikido in Europe.

"When Nakazono Sensei arrived, his Aikido was entirely different to what we had been taught," said Ellis. "Abbe Sensei didn't say this, but I'm sure he was surprised. There was a lot more movement. It resembled what we were doing, but there was far more movement."

According to Ellis, the members of the British clubs had always been taught by Abbe that resistance to the techniques was necessary and that do give less than 100 percent in attacks during practice was not at all appropriate.

"Abbe Sensei's Aikido was that of the early days and was more of a Ju Jutsu – we studied this religiously," said Ellis. "Anyway, we were told that when Nakazono Sensei arrived, we must practice the same way and must not give in to him, as this is a sign of disrespect to your teacher."

So when Nakazono came on the mat for the first time at The Hut, he was met with a crowd of strong Englishmen who were proud of their school and deeply respectful of their teachers and the lessons in early Aikido which had been taught to them. No one dared to do anything less than what Abbe had said.

Resistance to the techniques Nakazono was demonstrating was total -- but it was also fruitless.

"As we resisted Nakazono Sensei, he became increasingly angry," said Ellis. "Of course, the more angry he became, the more viscious his technique became, and obviously, there were more injuries. But we carried on resisting him, and he thought we were absolutely crazy."

During this time, no one told Nakazono about Abbe's request that the students resist as a show of respect.

"I don't think there was one Dan grade who went away from that seminar without an injury," said Ellis. "There were broken wrists, broken fingers, strained ligaments, dislocations -- we were not aware of what we were doing wrong, and we could not understand why the man had taken such a dislike to us. We thought it was him; we didn't realize it was us."

When the truth finally came to light, the students appologized to Nakazono, and more vigorous training began.

Eventually, Nakazono announced that all the students would have to be regraded.

"I kept my grade and so did the others," said Ellis. "But one Dan Grade was demoted from 2nd Dan to 1st Dan and told to 'sell his kit while the prices were high.' This didn't impress him much, and he was very unhappy for some considerable time. I think this destroyed him and it was later that he stopped training.

The reason was political. We later heard from Abbe Sensei that the Hombu did not want Western students progressing too highly at that time in the grading system, as it may undermine the authority of Japanese instructors.

The Salesmen

As Eastman and Ellis continued to practice, it was probably inevitable that the two of them would branch out into other areas along with Aikido, which only a year after its introduction, was beginning to really flourish.

Under Williams' direction, the two men travelled to other areas in Britain, giving demonstrations at various martial art clubs.

"We'd go out into other areas and try to carry on as many demonstrations as we could, so that the martial art would become known," said Ellis. "And it was surprising, because as many places as we went, no one had ever heard of Aikido. Even people practicing other martial arts did not know what Aikido was.

"So, after carrying out many demonstrations and offering to show many different clubs the art -- some were interested and some were not -- we began to feel in some instances, like door-to-door salesmen," said Ellis. "But as time went on, people began to see what Aikido was all about and interest began to increase. So much so, in fact, that many Judo clubs began to include it as part of their tuition."

The open minded attitude of the massive British Judo organizations didn't last long, though.

As the number of Aikido practitioners swelled and interest in the art began to encroach on the business at the Judo clubs, these clubs shut down their Aikido explorations to insulate themselves from the tidal wave of interest which was building around Aikido.

Still, Ellis and Eastman continued their travels, taking odd-jobs to provide money for each successive trip.

"So, once we started to travel, we eventually reached a stage where we'd visit a club which had gleaned some knowledge of Aikido through various demonstrations or summer schools and we would occassionally retrace our steps and call in at dojos we'd previously stopped at to see how they were doing," said Ellis. "As we showed interest in them, of course, these clubs would show interest in what we were doing. This was really when Aikido began to get off the ground.

"I've always thought that Mr. Eastman and I really started this development," said Ellis. "We gave up our time and it was very hard at first. If there were no students at first, there was no one to pay for classes. And if there was no one to pay for classes, we'd starve."

The men worked on a railroad for a time - a place often referred to as "The Railway of Death."

"This was a disused railway which was in the process of having the ties replaced," said Ellis, "and although this was a temporary job, these guys really wanted their money's worth.

"So, we slaved there for some time. It was hard. But fortunately for us, we could take every job lightly, because it was a means to an end. If we could feed ourselves for a day that was fine," said Ellis. "I think the longest we ever worked anywhere was for about a week."

One of the best jobs the two men ever had during this period, was working in a steel works.

"Because of our cheek and charm, we literally had the run of the place," said Ellis. "There were people who had worked there for 40 years and still, the directors totally ignored them. With us, however, they'd always stop and pass the time of day."

A lot of the jobs they'd take would last only briefly. Someone might say "can you make a gold watch?" Well, they may not have been able to make a gold watch -- but for the two hours they were there, they'd get two hours pay.

"So we'd do anything," said Ellis. "When I look back on this now, I really feel like it was one of the best times of my life. I was doing something I enjoyed -- money didn't really matter. If I had sufficient funds to eat, a place to sleep and could practice Aikido -- what more did I need?"

Another job the two men took to fund their continuing travels in Aikido, was a job as assistants to an undertaker. Whilst it was a fairly enjoyable job - as usual, they didn't stay long.

"You've seen the photograph of me and Derek in the top hats," said Ellis, "and I can assure you that in the coffin is, in fact, a lady of about 76 or so. Quite a sweet old lady, actually.

The job the two men had landed involved going back and forth from morgue to collect the bodies, then placing them in the Temple of Rest, which is located behind the two men in the photograph.

"The Temple of Rest actually holds some very fond memories for me," said Ellis, "as I laid a maiden to rest in that very place. In fact, that was one of the main reasons the funeral director didn't like me."

One final incident at the funeral home however, had the two men packed up and on the road again. Before that, however, Ellis made an interesting find at a local Aikido dojo.

The tradition of choosing an assistant dates itself back through dojo history. Good teachers have always needed someone they can trust to run the club in their absence - someone to whom they can pass the entire system to - or to whom they can turn to to demonstrate technique.

An assistant often gets much harsher treatment than other students, but the benefits are great as their learning is accelerated and thier abilities soon outstrip their fellow students. Today, the practice is carried on in some schools - but in many cases, this is informal , and doesn't carry the weight and meaning it once did.

Back in the mid to late 1960s, however, Ellis had not found a new assistant which measured up to the high marker Eastman had set.

Mad Geoff

"I never chose an assistant lightly. An assistant is someone very special – someone that will carry out a large number of duties," said Ellis. "Finding those qualities is rare, and it's rarer still in Aikido, where not only does the individual have to be strong, but he has to be able to take a great deal of punishment and keep coming back for more."

One such student was a man Ellis had met around the time he and Eastman were working as undertaker's assistants.

Jeff Goodwin was an extremely focused individual, intent on moving to the South and beginning training with Ellis.

"When you travel and teach Aikido, people will always come to you about the possibility of coming to train at headquarters with you," said Ellis. "This is always a nice, idle dream, but in this instance, Mr. Goodwin wanted to make this a reality. So, I did find accomodation and a job for him, making it possible for him to come down and study."

A year later, Goodwin was named assistant to Ellis.

"He turned out to be a very good assistant," said Ellis. "He was only the second assistant to me after Mr. Eastman, so you can imagine how good he had to be. He was excellent. Etiquette, training – you could smash him around and he always got up. He always came back. He was very good on knife and everything else – he trained and trained."

Ellis points out that stories about Mr. Goodwin are still told to this day. His nickname amongst the students was "Mad Geoff," due to his training on the mat, and his unceasing practice at home.

"He used to stay at home at night practicing with the knife and sword, cutting finer and closer to his body," said Ellis. "He lopped his ear almost off one night and I had to go to the hospital with him while he had it stitched back on. But he was on the mat the next night with the bandage wrapped around his head."

"I'm o.k., Sensei," Jeff had said. "No problem."

"He was that kind of guy – very serious," said Ellis. "An excellent student, and Chiba Sensei liked him very much. Jeff went on displays with Sensei and was assistant to him occasionally."

Jeff also attended many demonstrations with Ellis, and it was during one of these that Jeff came off the mat following a knife technique display with his teacher. Standing off the mat, next to Ellis' wife as another display began, Jeff stared out at the action on the mat.

"It's hard to watch that when you and Henry practice with the knife," said Mrs. Ellis. "I always think you're really trying to kill him."

Jeff turned his gaze on the woman. Eyes as flat black as those of a shark showed no emotion as Jeff answered.

"I am trying to kill him," he said. "If I can get that bastard, it will prove once and for all that I'm better than him."

Jeff stayed with the Ellis Schools for years, then disappeared.

About this time, an Aikido summer school was held where Ueyshiba's art was finally accepted on equal terms with Judo and Karate. Nakazono was the teacher to offer instruction in Aikido at this course, which lasted a week - through the student's vacations from work.

The regimen was three hours in the morning, three in the afternoon and three in the evening for the dan grades alone.

"This was a very hard course under Nakazono Sensei," said Ellis, "and this was our vacation. We trained very hard during the day which was three hours in the morning and three hours in the afternoon, but prior to the early morning, it was my job to take all the students on early morning running for four or five miles."

While Nakazono Sensei was named as the official European representative from the Aikikai, another Japanese visitor startled many of the British practitioners.

Masamichi Norro Sensei was a young, powerful teacher of Aikido just coming to the West from Japan. Wearing a white hakama, Norro surprised many of the dan grades – and not just because of his appearance.

"He was the most graceful Aikido teacher we'd ever seen," said Ellis. "Whereas Nakazon Sensei was very effective, Norro was so graceful."

It was Norro in fact, who introduced a system by which the huge number of Aikido techniques could be easily categorized – a method which was aimed at standardizing the requirements for Aikido students across Europe.

But with Aikido's rapid expansion, this attempt to provide some structure on which to base proper training and evaluation, was doomed to fail. Aikido continued its rapid expansion into the West undergoing massive changes along the way. While in the 1950s most practitioners knew Aikido was effective, today the question is routinely raised by other martial artists, members of the media and even people involved in the art.

Norro sensei was a strong exponent for Aikido in its early days. His system of categorization - a grouping of eight forms with eight techniques in each form, was intended for use as a way to easily evaluate students' performance while providing a tangible framework to ensure students practiced appropriately.

Many of the clubs in the U.K. during the early 1960s would adopt this system, but few would continue with it over time. As time went on and Aikido became more and more well-known, the technique of Ueyshiba's Aikido would be degraded by Westerners who would focus only on one aspect of the system or another.

Additionally, many of the early Dan grades were disgusted as "honorary" dan grades began to be handed out to civic leaders and those who had significantly helped with the promotion of Aikido in the United Kingdom.

"Now you have honorary titles in many fields," said Ellis, "but these people would never refer to themselves as 'honorary.'"

Ellis explained that the result of this practice was the further collapse of the martial art system.

"It's very difficult for me to discern where things started to go wrong," said Ellis, "but if I could put a finger on a particular area, it would be this one. All the other Dan grades felt the same about this – none of them liked it, and of course, the worse happened.

"The people who should have started their own clubs – the genuine Dan grades – did not do so," said Ellis. "It was the others – the "honorary" Dan grades – that started their own breakaway groups and began to teach. I don't have to mention names here, I'll just say that one of these latter individuals is now running one of the largest organizations in Britain."

Mr. Williams was a very powerful character, and he controlled all the Dan grades. Everybody was totally under his control. Nobody would have ever thought of opening a club of their own, taking a seminar on their own or anything, without asking his permission. Out of respect, you did not do it.

Even when people asked for something, everyone always said that it could be accomplished only through Mr. Williams. This built up his zone of control even more. He had complete control of Aikido for nearly 15 years. But as the honorary dan grades began to open clubs, and the real teachers left, Williams' lost control over the development of the art in Britain and splinter-groups began to form.

At this time in 1966, Ellis' longtime assistant, Derek Eastman, now a powerful practitioner of the martial art, married and moved to Basingstoke, Berkshire, where he opened another Aikido club with all the power and vitality of The Hut in the early days.

At this point, Ellis operated one dojo in Bracknell and two in SLough. He would often visit the Basingstoke club, however, due to the high standards Eastman continued to maintain.

"Derek's dojo became very strong and I then started to travel and visit the Basingstoke club. It was just like headquarters – the standard was exactly the same," said Ellis. "Mr. Eastman had three students there, David Warne, Kieth Webb and Ken Beake. These three were coming along really well and were the next line of Dan grades to come on the scene.

In all my years we've produced very few Dan grades, but the ones we have produced, have been of the highest standard. When Nakazono once told me that with my grade I could go practice at the Aikikai, that was a great compliment to me. Well, I always thought that if ever I was in a position to teach a student to Dan grade, I would like to think that they would be of the same caliber. I still believe that today."

As the 1960s rolled into the 1970s, Eastman's new Basingstoke club gained momentum, gathering more students all the time. David Warne, Kieth Webb and Ken Beak became teachers at the dojo, and acted as surrogate assistants to Ellis whenever he came to visit.

The next one to come up was Andy Lyon, who started in the early 80s and acted as Ellis' assistant for some time.

At the beginning of this time period, the United States and Russia were at the height of the cold war. As a doomsday system, the ground launched cruise missile system (GLCM) was moved into an old WWII British base just outside of Newbury, Berkshire, two young American servicemen began to attend classes at the Basingstoke club.

"This was a hard training club," said Ellis, "and not many people would stay in such an atmosphere. Only the most dedicated students would stay the course. Well, it didn't take too long to realize that the two American students, Dave Rogers and Al Montemar, would.

"We realized that these two students were worth some time and effort," said Ellis. "So I took Mr. Montemar as my personal assistant and trained him. And Dave Rogers became assistant to all the rest – which was probably worse, because they all smashed him in from one end to the other. He was the one student always available to one or another of the Dan grades."

The two servicemen continued training at Basingstoke until the GLCM system was eliminated by treaty with Russia and Greenham Common was shut down. Al Montemar returned to Dallas, Texas and Dave Rogers went back to Alamogordo where a new club was started in 1990.

Called "The Hut Combat Arts," after the original "Hut" in Britain, Rogers' new club began training members of the military and police forces as well as several Air Force dependents and local area civilians. In time, Alamogordo's "Hut" would develop a reputation for hard training and no-nonsense fighters.

In Dallas, Texas, Al Montemar would run a small club for awhile, but spent most of his time visiting other clubs and attending seminars. His technique and execution both powerful and flawless after training in Britain, he made both enemies and friends in an environment where most Aikido schools had turned into havens for people searching for themselves - or those who wanted to practice "play-fighting" where they wouldn't have to endure pain or actually fight.

Indeed, this "new-age" movement of Aikido continues todaythroughout the world, with clubs focusing on "cooperation" instead of effective martial technique. And while this seems to be a profitable course to follow now, it brings into serious question the validity and future of a martial art once fit for kings.

Oral tradition

The contents of this section includes:

The "Dodgy-man"
A martial flower blossoms
The "Chindit"
A difficult seminar
A long walk home
Discipline is universal
The Demonstration
Best memories
More remembered

Sensei Derek Eastman prepares to pin his son, Mark eastman after intercepting an attack with the knife.

In martial art history many legends exist. These are partly due to the fact that most people enjoy a well-told story; but it is also due to the fact that generation after generation of teachers have passed these stories down from teacher to student. Sometimes, the point of these tales is difficult to grasp - perhaps there are instances when there is no real meaning.

But often, the tales are meant to illustrate a particular idea – like lights along a path at night, they serve to show us possible directions we can take in our training and our lives. I will offer some relatively modern stories here, as told by my teachers. While these may appear to be of questionable value at times, I have often used them on the mat to help in the instruction of today's students.

The "Dodgy-man"

LESSON LEARNED: Nicknames may be well placed, but earning them can be painful.

When Ellis and Eastman were traveling on the weekends, attending courses, Nakazono Sensei was made the official European Representative from the Aikikai.

Also at that time, there was a new young protege from the Aikikai who is now the Paris representative of the Aikikai. That was Norro Sense.

"We all liked Norro," said Ellis, "and to this day, if I saw him now, he'd probably call me "Dodgy-man."

"I don't know what the American word is for "dodgy," but another British word for it is "shifty.""

According to Ellis, his nickname by Norro was the result of the break-up of a relationship he had with a young British woman.

"Mr. Williams had asked me if I'd heard from this young lady," said Ellis. "So I said 'Well, I'd just had a letter from her this morning.' Well, he read the letter and she was very sad, because she was heartbroken – which is normal. Mr. Williams said to Norro, 'Sensei, Mr. Ellis is a very dodgy man.' Well, Norro looked at him and said, 'Dodgy man. I understand.' This conversation was then all forgotten."

The next day at the seminar the members of the school were all very much afraid of Norro, because he had such powerful technique. After starting the class, the Japanese teacher pointed his finger at Ellis and said "come out."

Taking Ellis into a powerful shihonage technique, Norro stopped halfway through, holding Ellis' arm in a painful grip before the throw.

"He just looked me straight in the eyes and said, 'Ahh, dodgy man,'" said Ellis. "And as he threw me, and I was in pain, he said, "That is for the young lady.""

From that day on Norro always called Ellis "Dodgy man."

"He was quite a charmer too," said Ellis, "and a great character. He made many visits to England."

A martial flower blossoms
LESSON LEARNED: Beer requires sacrifice.

At the first British summer school where Aikido was accepted as an equal with other martial arts, Nakazono Sensei came to visit.

"It was during one particular practice that we had two students there who were very big in size," said Ellis. "One of them had turned to the other one who was much bigger than him and said, 'You could resist Nakazono Sensei, because you're so big and he's so small.' So the big one assured the small one that he in fact could not. He said, 'Look Morris, I know you think I can, but I can't. However, if you think you can, feel free to try.'"

"So Morris, being a prat (fool), tried," said Ellis, and he finished up with every finger of one hand broken. That was the end of his summer course for him, and also the end of his career in Aikido. I've seen him, but he's never practiced since."

This was a very hard course under Nakazono Sensei, and this was most of the students' vacation.

"We trained very hard during the day which was three hours in the morning and three hours in the afternoon, but prior to the early morning, it was my job to take all the students on early morning running for four or five miles," said Ellis.

When they came back after the run, they would shower, have breakfast, rest for about an hour, then start training. Later, about eight or ten Dan grades would be instructed by Nakazono Sensei to go back on the mat from 7 to 10 p.m.

"If you can imagine training all this time during the day, then spending all that time training at night, you can imagine, we were horrified at this," said Ellis. "Being wise, however, we didn't say anything."

At this time, Mr. Williams was the national coach, and he asked Ellis to have a word with Nakazono Sensei to "tell him this was our holiday, and we'd like to finish at 9 p.m."

"Well, the fact was, we didn't even want to practice at all in the evening," said Ellis. "We'd had enough. So, a small practice would have been sufficient. Well, Mr. Williams wouldn't ask him; so I did."

Catching Nakazono after a practice, Ellis politley asked the teacher his question.

"Would it be possible to finish at 9 p.m., as we'd like to change and go up to the pub before the evening is over," he said.

And it was then that he realized why I had been made to ask this.

"He just went absolutely mad and screamed at me that he'd come all the way from the other side of the world to teach Aikido and all we wanted to do as Dan grades was go to the pub and drink beer," said Ellis. "Well, the way he said it, it sounded terrible. But I was on the other side. I was the one who was suffering from hard training and the need for English Koku (beer). So, without further comment, we carried on and trained until 10 p.m. It was a matter of tucking your hakama into your socks as it were, and running up to the pub – something we'd never done before. But if we'd have changed, we'd never have made the pub."

The Chindit
LESSON LEARNED: No humming on the mat

During the time Ellis and Eastman were working as undertakers assistants, they were also teaching at the dojo in Nottinghamshire.

"There was a large dojo there with a very good class of students," said Ellis. "But of course they weren't up to the standards of headquarters. And in those days, I was young, strong and arrogant. So I went in to teach these people."

There were 37 students on the first night's practice but after a week the club had been whittled down to only three people.

"The only thing that I can say about that is that we had three good students left," said Ellis. "In retrospect now, I think that, yes, I was too hard, but we did have a lot of guys in this club that tried it on and suffered the consequences. We had quite a few injuries."

This was also the dojo where the Chindit man was.

"On my very first night's visit to this dojo, we were all in the dressing room changing and there's this Custer-like character with a long, droopy mustache and a chindit hat on his head, pipe in his mouth. And he got changed without taking off his hat or his pipe," said Ellis. "Then he put on his gi and got all ready to go on the mat."

The man then went on the mat and nobody told Ellis or Eastman, who was also there, that he was a little strange.

"I thought he was strange," said Ellis, "but then, this was a strange part of Britain, anyway. It was similar to traveling in the backwoods of New Mexico or Texas."

During the class, Ellis and Eastman were teaching, and the mat was absolutely packed solid. A student couldn't be thrown without the dan grades stopping everyone on a section of mat and clearing an area. It was at this point Ellis heard a quiet, but very nice piece of humming.

"I remember the tune," said Ellis, "but I just can't remember the name of it.

"Well, I asked Derek who the hell was humming," said Ellis. "I didn't allow people to even speak while I was teaching, never mind hum."

Eastman said, "No one's humming Sensei!"

"Oh yes they are," said Ellis. "You get around that mat, find them and stop them."

So Eastman went one direction and Ellis went the other, and it was Ellis who caught the humming Chindit.

"I told him not to hum on the mat and he said he was sorry," said Ellis. "Well, he was doing the technique wrong – it was Nikkyo. Strange, but that was my favorite technique back then. So I decided to show the humming Chindit what Aikido was. So as I took him in Nikkyo, he did something that no one has ever done to me before. He actually started to stand back up.

"But I was being kind to him," said Ellis. "As you may know, I'm a very kind man."

"Well, as he came back up, not only did he resist me, but he started "Blue Moon" again. So I immediately, without even thinking, put nikkyo on 100 percent. And if you can imagine someone humming along and then finishing in a scream, that's what it was like. I broke his wrist totally. Understand, I'm not proud of this, but all I can say is that it stopped his humming," said Ellis. "And, I'm afraid that was the end of the Chindit-man."

A difficult seminar
LESSON LEARNED: Don't bring your problems into the dojo.

In the early 1960's Derek Eastman was assistant to Henry Ellis, and it was at this time that he went to the ancient city of Norwich to attend a week-long National Seminar.

"This was probably the biggest event in the martial arts calendar in those early day's," said Eastman.

Kenshiro Abbe sensei and Matsuro O'Tani Sensei were tteaching Judo, Tomio O'Tani teaching Kendo, with Harada Sensei teaching Karate. The Aikido was being taught by the National Coach Ken Williams and his assistant Henry Ellis.

"Subsequently, this looked as if it was going to be a great week as I arrived with my two friends Trevor Jones who was another senior Aikido assistant and Ken Waite who was the assistant to Harada Sensei," said Eastman.

Unfortunately things went wrong at the beginning of the week when Trevor started speaking to some local girls.

"Their boyfriends took a dim view of this and tried to start a fight," said Eastman, "but because this was such a high profile seminar, we decided to make a discreet retreat. Unfortunately, the trouble followed us back to the martial arts centre."

This was a time when Ellis Sensei was one of the hardest teachers of positive Aikido, and so he confronted the three men in the lobby area and demanded to know why they had retreated instead of standing their ground and "sorting the other guys out."

"To my total astonishment, Trevor answered Sensei back," said Eastman. "Without turning his body, Sensei hit Trevor with his now famous back hand atemi. That was the first time Trevor had given Sensei any lip and it was definitely the last."

According to Eastman, the three men were all feeling pretty miserable for a while, but an incident the next day cheered the three up a great deal.

"Ellis Sensei was always one for the ladies," said Eastman, "and this young women with the biggest pair of frontal techniques you could ever hope to see, was showing him a great deal of interest. So Sensei invited her back to the twin bedded room that he shared with Williams Sensei – are you ready for this one – to iron his Hakama.

"Sensei was always a meticulous sort of guy, and as his bed was so neat and tidy, he used Sensei Williams bed," said Eastman. "When Sensei Williams saw the state of his bed he almost went berserk, and as we went back for the next three hour session, we could see that Sensei Williams was still on the boil. Every technique that he demonstrated, he would smash Sensei Ellis through the mat."

"The three of us sat on the edge of the mat and thoroughly enjoyed every moment," said Eastman. "Trevor was constantly nudging me with his elbow, obviously savoring the display."

A long walk home
LESSON LEARNED: Sometimes it's better to just shut up.

Although Trevor Jones did not answer Sensei Ellis back ever again, he did have a way of upsetting him.

On one occasion Ellis was driving back from a Seminar. In the car with him were Eastman, Jones, and a couple others.

"We were on the other side of London and there were five of us in the car when Trevor started to complain about Sensei's driving," said Eastman. "He was told very firmly to shut up, but a little while later he complained again. This time Sensei suddenly pulled into the side of the road and told Trevor to get out. Trevor protested that we were a long way from home and he had no money. Sensei told him he had five seconds to get out of his car, otherwise he would be physically thrown out. Trevor decided the wise move was to get out and hope that Sensei would think he had taught him a lesson and let him back in the car. But as Trevor shut the door, Sensei drove off and left him.

"Remember, these stories are still about Aikido training – the training was not only on the mat but off it," said Eastman. "With Sensei everything was about etiquette and discipline, and he was probably harder on himself than the students."

Discipline is universal
LESSON LEARNED: Respect is earned and must be maintained.

At the end of the National Martial Arts display in London around 1962, a judo teacher from a large dojo in the Nottingham area walked up to Ellis and told him how impressed he was with the Aikido demonstration. The teacher invited the two men to spend a weekend with him and teach at his dojo.

"When we arrived he told us that our reputation for very strict discipline was well known and then told us that we could not expect that kind of discipline in the north of England," said Eastman.

Ellis asked "why?"

The man then explained that his students were much stronger and tougher than the people of the South. They were coal miners and steel workers and involved in other heavy industries that the North was noted for. Ellis then said he did not understand the analogy, and irrespective of his occupation, a man is still a man.

"When we arrived at the dojo we were shocked to find the place was more like a social club, with students wandering around chatting, walking on and off the mat at will," said Eastman. "When their Sensei walked on the mat they were slapping him on the back and there was absolutely no respect at all. Sensei told me to go on the mat and very firmly line the class up in grades and make them sit up with backs straight. As I knelt on the mat I just stared straight ahead."

Ten minutes later Ellis came out, but the silence made it seem like hours to Eastman.

"As Sensei knelt in front of the class, he looked at each student for a moment from one end of the line to the other, then snapped 'sit up correctly.' From that time on, it was just like being in our own dojo," said Eastman. "The judo teacher asked so many times over the weekend 'how did you do that', I was on the mat and you also had me under your strict discipline."

The Demonstration

LESSON LEARNED: Sometimes the right way is the wrong way.

Sometime after 1960.

Two young Englishmen wait to give a demonstration of Aikido, a martial art which is still relatively new to the West after it's release to the general public in 1955.

The venue for this demonstration is an important one, with serious ramifications for the future of Aikido. Subsequently, the two men were handpicked by the great and respected teacher, Kenshiro Abbe Sensei to provide this demonstration in front of Lady Baden Powell and the Japanese Ambassador.

Powell, the wife of Lord Baden-Powell who was the head of the World Organization of Boy Scouts, was seated in the front row nearest the stage as the two men spoke to Masutaro Otani and Abbe Sensei.

Abbe and Otani repeatedly stressed the importance of the display, and the need to demonstrate it precisely and with an eye toward keeping it low-key and gentle, so as not to scare or offend Lady Baden-Powell.

The men both nodded their heads respectfully.

"Of course, Sensei," said the first man, Henry Ellis.

"We'll be very careful, Sensei," said the other, a young man by the name of Derek Eastman.

While the two were waiting to go out on stage for the demonstration, however, a Judo Dan Grade approached Otani who was speaking to the Japanese Ambassador.

"Hey Smiler," the man said.

An expression of amazement flashed across the face of Ellis as he heard this remark, then his face hardened as he took off in pursuit of the Judo practitioner who was walking away. As the two exchanged harsh words by the side of the stage, Eastman, who had been out smoking a cigarette, came over to tell Ellis they were about to be called to go on stage.

The two men then rushed to the stage, Ellis still angry over the earlier incident.

As the first technique was applied, Estman hit the mat, but not before his cigarettes and matches fell out of his gi onto the tatami..

Ellis, angry before stepping on the mat, was now furious, and as he took the next technique, began smashing his partner from one side of the mat to the other.

The demonstration had now become a battle.

When it came time for knife technique, Eastman took hold of the blade and attacked Ellis wildly. Already moving, Ellis was shocked when he felt the blade tear through his gi.

"My God, it's in me," he thought, as he quickly dropped to his knees and place Eastman in immobilization.

Slowly withdrawing the blade from his gi, Ellis was surprised to find no blood. The knife had narrowly missed him, although his gi was mortally wounded. Looking up, he was just in time to see the look of unabashed horror on the face of Lady Baden Powell who was seated just a few feet away from him.

Any hope of securing her sponsorship for Aikido had disappeared in the few intense minutes it had taken for the demonstration.

When asked about the demonstration later, her ladyship would be quoted as saying, "That was the most horrific display of violence I have ever witnessed." And while her ladyship didn't congratulate Ellis and Eastman, the Japanese Ambassador did.

Shaking the hands of the two Westerners, the Ambassador smiled, "That was an excellent display," he said.

Best memories
By Derek Eastman Sensei
Concerning the first time he entered the Abbe School of Budo ("The Hut")

LESSON LEARNED: Sometimes the odd beating is easier to take than learning a martial art

In 1959 myself and a few friends, all motorcyclists very much in the style of Marlon Brando in "The Wild Ones," were all around 16-years-old. We'd decided to learn Judo so we could "beat up" the regiment of guards who would regularly give us a thrashing at the coffee bars on the river Thames at Windsor.

We knew Judo was taught behind a pub called "The Hut" in West Drayton, just west of London, so we roared up to the pub to become tough guys.

Although Judo was at that time, paramount, we turned up during a session of "Aikido." This was a special class drawn from Judoka at the club to form a nucleus of instructors. After watching the students overcoming various 100 percent attacks by each other, we were told a beginner's class would be starting soon and we all immediately signed up.

I did not know at this time that a Mr. Henry Ellis had been recently awarded 1st Dan Aikido and was to be the instructor of this first true beginner's class held at The Hut. In retrospect, I think it would have been much less painful to suffer the odd beating given to myself by the guards, than when attending those two-hour sessions of this first class.

Achieving a training certificate in Aikido

When I first started to train in Sensei Ellis' class in 1959, it was just to keep fit and be able to defend myself better than I could.

It was soon apparent that there is no easy way to achieve this, except by hard training – something made evident in all the clubs belonging to the British Judo Council founded by Master Kenshiro Abbe.

However, this was never more true than it was at "The Hut."

Whether Judo, Karate, Kendo or Aikido, all trained hard – particularly in Sensei Ellis' classes.

After less than six weeks, Sensei Ellis asked me to be his assistant. It was with great trepidation that I said "yes." Being an assistant involved special training in helping to care for the dojo and taking the class exercises. Although Sensei Ellis would exercise with the class and then carry on with more.

This first class consisted of at least 20 students whose living was as professional doormen at the night clubs in West London. This made for a very physical class.

People who visit the Hut today find it hard to believe that 40 to 60 students could train in such a small dojo. You did not lie there after being thrown, or you would be injured by another falling body. This taught tight Ukemi, often making the Uke able to attack again before Nage could prepare.

Demonstration before a top teacher

LESSON LEARNED: Sometimes the right way is the right way.

October 23, 1965.

It's a Saturday afternoon at the National Recreation Center in Britain as two young men step somewhat nervously onto a large wrestling mat inside the facility.

There for a demonstration of the traditional Japanese martial art of Aikido, the two men only now realized that they would be demonstrating their skills before the world-famous Karate master Tatsuo Suzuki, 8th Dan.

This day, Suzuki would be showcasing the powerful techniques of Wado Ryu Karate, but not untill the two young Englishmen had finished their demonstration of Aikido.

The Aikido display began as it usually did - with nice, clean technique, but just a few minutes into the display, the attacker, Derek Eastman, did something to upset his partner, Sensei Henry Ellis.

Subsequently, the demonstration became nasty.

After smashing his opponent into the mat, Ellis was rewarded with the usual response -Eastman went berserk and the display became a battle.

After finishing the demonstration, the men stepped to the edge of the mat, only to find Suzuki Sensei coming straight towards them.

Glaring sternly ar Ellis, Suzuki stopped right in front of him and looked him straight in the eyes. Then he bowed and held out his hand.

Nervously shaking the Karate master's hand, Ellis was astonished as Suzuki said, "Thank you. That was the best display of Aikido I have ever seen."

One is all it takes

LESSON LEARNED: One is all it takes.

Sometime after 1970

In the early 1970s, Derek and I visited a dojo in Winchester. We arrived in the middle of the evening and about 35 students were just coming off the mat for a coffee break. We asked permission to go on the mat, and we were offered coffee before going on. We declined, and after a while, only 15 of the students came back on the mat. They were Tomiki Style and very soft.

The instructor asked me to take the class , but the students didn't seem to understand even our most basic technique. After the class we all went to the pub for the customary pint of beer.

While having a drink with Derek and their instructor, one of the brown belts came over and asked his teacher, "Sensei, what do you think is the main difference between Sensei Ellis' technique and ours?"

The teacher said, "Whereas Sensei Ellis does one technique, I would interchange between six to possibly eight techniques."

"Sensei, I would agree with that," the student then said to me. "Why do you only use one technique when my teacher would use several?"

I replied, "I only need one."

– Sensei Henry Ellis

More remembered

LESSON LEARNED: This is a way of life.

We started the Basingstoke Aikido Club in 1970 at the Sports Center in Basingstoke, Hampshire, eventually persuading Sensei Ellis to visit and become our principal instructor.

The students, always few in number, have always been well received.

To meet with European directives on martial arts, we formed the Ellis School of Traditional Aikido and joined the British Aikido Board of the Martial Arts Commission in our own right.

We have instructed at several USA Air Force bases over the years. The most recent and adjacent to Basingstoke was the USAF at RAF Greenham Common. There we started a small club with Al Montemar and David Rogers, along with about six others. We used this as an extension of the Basingstoke club, and it was a good class at both.

When the base was closing, we were asked to perform a demonstration there in front of the command office.

Sensei Henry Ellis takes technique on Geoff Goodwin inSlough 1967.

Instead of Sensei Ellis and myself giving the demonstration, which was well attended, Al Montemar and David Rogers demonstrated the techniques – myself being Uke to them. This was very well received and respected by martial artists in the audience as they showed the technique they had received – it was not just an act.

In 30 years, the Basingstoke Aikido Club has gained Dan grades with Ken Beak, David Warne, Keith Webb, Andy Lyon and Mark Eastman. Along with Al Montemar and David Rogers of the USAF, perhaps this is too few. But each could practice equally with my instructors at those early days of Aikido instruction in England.

I can only add that the very best memories are of the teachers and fellow students along the way; assisting the masters visiting Master Kenshiro Abbe – even sometimes just transporting them to and fro.
• Masutaru Otani and his three sons; all fine Judo and Kendo practitioners.
• Tadashe Abbe, Matsuhara Nakazono, Masamichi Norro – all representing the Aikikai.
• Master Ken Williams, whose influence in spreading Aikido throughout the United Kingdom was enormous.
• Master Haydon Foster, who would have a throaty chuckle as he put you two feet below the tatami.
• Eric Dollimore who had a great influence on Sensei Ellis one day by putting him through two partitioning walls of The Hut.
• Peter Dowden and Lennie Ballard who specialized in teaching women – I still teach their techniques to allow women to practice equally with men.
• John Caldwood, a professional boxer whom when I thought I could handle anyone, put me in the boxing ring and I did not remember leaving.
• My sensei Henry Ellis – by far the best to accept knife techniques I have ever seen.
• I trained alongside Trevor Jones, Les White, Ron James, Andy Allen, Hamish McFarlane – all who have now trained fine students.
As well as remaining close friends with Master Henry Ellis, it was also good to see his son Richard and my son Mark practicing together from 12-years-old till now.

With respect to those mentioned and my sensei, Henry Ellis.
Derek Eastman.

Students today take all that there is for them in Aikido for granted, I will tell you of just one guy who was the first dan grade from outside of the Hut, although he trained at the Hut.

In the 1950's the first " Aikido visitor" from outside our local area was a Judo man all the way from Birmingham, a man by the name of Ralph Reynolds, Ralph would drive down from Birmingham long before there were any motorways (Interstate highways) which would make this a very tiresome journey.

He would arrive early on a Sunday morning after a three hour drive, often before the local lads appeared.he often helped the dojo assistant Derek Eastman to prepare the dojo for the Sunday morning practice.
He would learn as much as he could absorb, then go back to teach a few students in the Midland City of Birmingham.
It would be fair to say that Birmingham today is the hub of British Aikido and much of the credit goes to Ralph Reynolds.

As Mr Reynolds was pushing the progress of Aikido in the Midlands, Sensei Williams wanted the progress to move much faster, he decided to create some honoury dan grades to fill the gap, there was a guy I did not really know in Newcastle in the North of England, and another in Wales that were given honoury dan grades to act as Aikido figure heads in their area's , even the landlord of the Hut public house received one. the old dan grades felt betrayed, the reason that Aikido had progressed as successfully as it had was due to the high standard set by the dan grades, we asked " what will people make of these new dan grades".

The great comaderie at the Hut seemed to break down, I can't honestly put my finger on the button that started the decline, but my first guess would be the affore mentioned problems

- Henry Ellis.

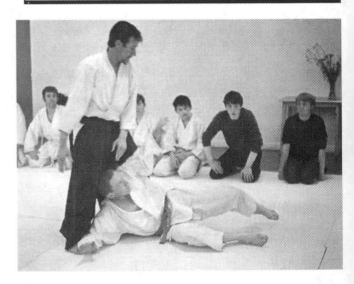

I had been asked to take Kenshiro Abbe Sensei and Bill Woods Sensei to London Airport where they would fly to Franceto teach several seminars. As I arrived, Bill was getting the last bags together ready to leave, Abbe sensei made some small talk with me, I said that I was booked to fly to Spain the next day with my girlfriend and my parents, I explained that my father had been in extreme back pain for two weeks, I also explained that we would not be able to go. Abbe asked "where does your father live Henry" I told him that my father lived in BracknellinBerkshire. Abbe sensei turned to Bill Woods and said " Mr Woods, where is Bracknelland how long will it take to get there?" Bill replied " Sensei, Brack-nellis at least 20 miles the other side of the Airport" Abbe Sensei then asked if we could make a visit to my father and still make the flight toParis? " Bill was getting a little agitated and replied that we did not have time.

Abbe Sensei looked sternly at Bill as if he had made his mind up. "Mr Woods, we must hurry and see Henry's father" . I drove as fast as possible from Acton London to Bracknell Berkshire. some 40/50 miles.

When we arrived at my parents home where my father was lying on a wooden door on the bed, and unable to move, he was amazed to see Abbe Sensei walk into the bedroom, Abbe Sensei indicated we all leave the room. after just a few minutes the bedroom door opened and out walked my father, a little unsteady at first, soon he was walking the full length of the long hallway. Abbe Sensei said " OK, airport quickly."

I drove like a bat out of hell for the airport where Abbe Sensei caught his flight on time.

My father was fine and never ever had another problem with his back, and we also made our vacation to Spain.

- Sensei Henry Ellis

Abbe Sensei hadbeen teaching at the Hut Dojo one day around 1961, and after practice Sensei Williams asked me to take Abbe Sensei back to his home inActon. Sensei Williams knew that I was nearly as mad a driver as Mr Ellis, he gave me a long lecture on what would happen to me if anything ever happened to Abbe sensie.

This was the first time I had given Abbe Sensei a lift in my BMW Isetta 3 wheeled "bubble" car.

This little two seater car with a full frontal opening door must have seemed really strange to Abbe Sensei. as I opened the door he looked at the Bubble car a little apprehensively . he climb in without another word, after a little while he said " Errgh Mr Eastman, this car , how many wheels?." I replied "Three sensei." he look concerned, then said "WHERE ARE WHEELS" I then replied "Sensei, there are two at the front, and one at the back" he seemed to relax and said " Ahhhhh that is good balance like trian-gle". he never spoke another word all the way home.

- Sensei Derek Eastman

When I was a student of Judo I was aware of Mr Foster who would come along and watch his son in the junior judo class who was also named Hayden. when I joined the Aikido section Mr Foster was a 5th kyu (Yellow belt) we trained a lot together and we became good friends, he was a little older than me, and in those days you would respect people who were older than you. although he was only a yellow belt he would teach me all he had learned, there has been many disputes in aikido yet Mr Foster and I have never ever had a disagreement in almost 50 years and we are still the best of friends, I have always called him the godfather of the Hut. There are only four survivors of the original group of students from the 1950's excluding Sensei Williams , I am still in constant touch with those four who are all good solid trusted friends Sensei's Hayden Foster, Eric Dollimore, Ralph Reynolds, Derek Eastman.

- Sensei Henry Ellis

Kenshiro Abbe Sensei wasa passenger in a car traveling down a High Street in West London when the car came to a halt in a traffic jam. Abbe Sensei looked down the street to see what was causing the traffic hold up, and the commotion just ahead of them. as he stepped from the vehicle he could see a police officer standing alongside a large redLondonbus, with a large Alsation dog at his feet. It appeared that the bus had run over and crushed the legs and lower body of the dog. The dog was in a great deal of pain and distress with no hope of survival. The large crowd of onlookers did nothing.

Abbe Sensei walked over to the police officer and indicated towards the dog, the Police officer nodded as if understanding the Japanese gentleman. Abbe dropped onto one knee next to the dog which was howling in great pain, he placed his hand gently on the dogs head, to every ones amazement the dog relaxed and became totally quiet, Abbe then made a very slight movement of the hand and the dog was dead. The police officer looked at Abbe Sensei and exclaimed "I don't know who you are sir, but that is the most compas-sionate thing I have ever witnessed". Abbe Sensei simply nodded and walked back to the car, he got back into the car without another word on the incident.

- Sensei Derek Eastman.

I will never forget the time I went to visit Abbe Sensei at the home he shared with Otani Sensei in Stuart Road Acton, London. I knocked on the door to his room, he called for me to enter, as I entered, the room had the usual variation of wild birds, there were pidgeons starlings and sparrows on the table and furniture.

This was not at all unusual, what was unusual to me was that Sensei was watching "Cricket" a very old and boring British game. as a young man, I was so disappointed to see this man that in our eyes was god like. to be watching this game, I politely asked "Sensei ! do you like cricket? " he looked at me sharply and replied " NO, THIS IS A VERY STUPID GAME" . I took a step backwards and nervously asked " Sensei, if you think it is stupid, why do you watch it?" he replied " This is the WORLD series, I watch every day, and still cannot understand this stupid game, they say world series, yet only countries that have been colonized by the British Empire play this stupid game. I thought that was very profound.

- Sensei Henry Ellis.

The teachers

On the following pages are some short biographies of the teachers who have influenced our school's technique.

This information was collected and compiled by Andy Lyon, 3rd Dan ESTA.

"There is nothing wrong or bad about any of the various martial arts; and if there is a problem, then it is only the idiots who practice it that bring it into disrepute."

-Sensei Henry Ellis

It is possible to see that in a given motion, all three aspects are in play. Flexibility (acceptance or redirection), immobility and pure offense all play a part in combat at any level. Without the aspect of the circle, we must either enter or remain in place. Without the triangle, we must only escape or remain in place.
Without the square there is no opportunity for structure or strength and subsequently, there can be no gaps or spaces in the fight – and no chance for rest. This is why when a martial artist says he practices only linear, hard technique, he or she is fooling themselves. Without all three elements, they would be a failure as a fighter. All true fighting methods incorporate all three aspects. But this also means something else – all martial artists are bound together as brothers and sisters, because the very things which define us as warriors connect us as surely as if we were siblings by blood.

O'Sensei Morihei Ueshiba

Aikido began with Master Morihei Uyeshiba, who instructed only to carefully selected students, requiring the highest references. Uyeshiba, known throughout the world as O'Sensei (Great Teacher), studied the Japanese Martial Arts of: Kito Ryu, Aioi Ryu, Daito Ryu, Aiki Jitsu, several other schools of JuJitsu and Judo. He also studied the bayonet arts, Kendo, Kyudo, bojitsu and many others. Aikido was created by Uyeshiba in the 1930s.

O'Sensei was such a powerful martial artist that he attracted students from all over Japan, including senior students of Kodokan Judo who were sent to him by Jigaro Kano Sensei, the creator of modern Judo.

Before the 2nd World War, Aikido was not taught to the general public, but after the war, the creator of Aikido decided that the martial art should be spread throughout Japan and the world.

O'Sensei died in 1969 at the age of 88. His son, Kisshomaru Uyeshiba took his place as the second headmaster of Aikido. Kisshomaru Uyeshiba died in 1999.

Sensei Kazuo Chiba

Sensei Kazuo Chiba practiced Judo and Karate before studying Aikido under O'Sensei.

When Sensei Kenshiro Abbe returned to Japan in 1964, he visited O'Sensei and asked him to send an instructor to England. In 1966, Sensei Kazuo Chiba was sent to Great Britain as an official Aiki Kai (World Headquarters) representative.

Shortly after Sensei Chiba arrived in the United Kingdom, Sensei Williams left the United Kingdom to study Aikido under Sensei Koichi Tohei, who had moved to the United States.

Sensei Ellis stayed in the U.K. and in 1968, he became the Assistant Coach for Aikido under the direction of Sensei Kazuo Chiba. Under Sensei Chiba's direction, Aikido spread increasingly over the United Kingdom.

Chiba Sensei's Aikido was fast, dynamic and powerful.

In 1976, Sensei Chiba returned to Japan, then later moved to San Diego, California, where he still lives and teaches as one of the most respected Aikido teachers in the world.

On Sensei Kazuo Chiba:

Abbe Sensei had not consulted Ken Williams Sensei, who was the first person to study Aikido in the U.K., and was by then, the National Coach for Aikido as appointed by Abbe Sensei and accepted by the Aiki Kai as their official representative. Williams Sensei and his dan grades had worked hard from absolutely nothing to what was a strong, national Aikido following. Williams Sensei was simply told that Chiba Sensei would now be in control of all Aikido in the U.K. As one can imagine, Chiba Sensei arrived to a very hostile reception from the Aikido community. Chiba Sensei was a young man of 26 years and very strong.

It was at this time that I resigned as Assistant National Coach and broke away from Sensei Williams' organization. I had two dojos in Slough, Buckinghamshire. One in Bracknell, Berkshire and another at the prestigious "Times" newspaper, in blackfriers district of London. I subsequently gave the London dojo to Chiba Sensei, and later, he opened another dojo at Earls Court, London.

As Chiba Sensei's assistant, I took part in many seminars, television appearances and also a 30-minute talk show on BBC World Service radio.

Sensei Kenshiro Abbe

One of O'Sensei's outstanding students was Sensei Kenshiro Abbe.

From an early age, Abbe had trained in all the Budo Arts. Born in 1916, he began Judo at 14 years of age, showing a talent of such a high degree that after two years, he was 2nd Dan.

In 1932 at age 16, he became the Japan High School Champion in the Judo League of Tokushima, also gaining his 3rd Dan. By 1934, he had reached 5th Dan, and at age 18, this made him the youngest ever to achieve this rank. During this period he was at the Budo College in Kyoto, coming first in graduation and also winning the top trophy in the "All-Japan -East West Contest" as well as winning the Imperial Contest for 5th Dan grades.

Sensei Abbe was also the youngest and later, the oldest man ever to have won the All Japan Judo Championships.

On graduation from the Budo College, Sensei Abbe became instructor to the Osaka Police, the High School of Kyoto and the special Judo College of Butokukwai, Japan's premier center of study for all the Martial Arts (founded in 1895). In 1938 at 23-years-old, he was the youngest ever to attain 6th Dan. In 1945 he was promoted to 7th Dan, becoming chief instructor to the Kyoto Police and Doshima University in 1949.

His studies of the other fighting arts were just as remarkable.

Training in Aikido under O'Sensei for a period of 10 years, he gained the rank of 6th Dan. He was also 5th Dan Karate and 5th Dan Kendo, and held Dan grades in Kyudo (archery) and Ju-Kenjitsu (bayonet fighting). Sensei Abbe came to England in 1955 at the age of 40. He founded the British Judo Council and later the International Budo Council in 1958.

He was the first to teach Aikido in the United Kingdom.

Abbe Sensei studied Aikido in the Pre-war years, and his practice methods reflected this with great emphasis on physical conditioning and strong technique.

When Abbe Sensei first introduced Aikido in the U.K., he chose Ken Williams Sensei as his first student. Williams Sensei was at that time, a 2nd Dan in Karate and 3rd Dan in Judo. He became the first National Coach for Aikido and selected Henry Ellis as his assistant, later becoming Assistant National Coach. Ellis Sensei was also a student of Karate and Judo.

Sensei Mitsusuke Harada

Sensei Mitsusuke Harada started training in Karate when he was 14-years-old at the Shotokan School in Tokyo. This included instruction under Gichin Funakoshi, the originator of modern Karate.

Sensei Harada studied at Wasada University and after graduation with a 5th Dan, he became the Karate teacher there. Following WWII, he taught Karate to the USAF at the Kodokan in Tokyo.

He later taught in Brazil for seven years, coming to Europe in 1963. After teaching in France and Belgium, he came to England and became the chief instructor of Karate to the International Budo Council.

Today, Sensei Harada is still an active karateka, and amongst the world's most respected Masters. He heads the Shotokai Karate organization.

Sensei harada was a regular visitor to the "Hut" in the United Kingdom, and Sensei Henry Ellis studied Karate with him and would teach him Aikido.

The results of this exchange were adjustments in both men's technique.

Sensei Derek Eastman also studied with Sensei Harada, and adapted the punching and kicking into the positive style of Aikido presently taught in the Ellis School.

On Sensei Mitsusuke Harada: Harada Sensei was a regular visitor to the "Hut." I Studied Karate with him and would teach him Aikido, and he would work some of the movement of Aikido into his Karate and I would use some of Sensei's Shotokai style in my Aikido.

On Sensei Kenshiro Abbe:
I had to collect Abbe Sensei to take him to a seminar. At this time, Sensei was living in the home of Otani Sensei in Acton, London. When I arrived, I was sent to Abbe Sensei's room. As I walked in, I could see that the windows were wide open and there were pigeons and other wild birds flying around the room. What surprised me most, however, was that this man I admired so much – this great Master, whom I looked upon almost as a God, was watching the "World Series" for Cricket. I just stared in disbelief.
"Why are you watching Cricket," I asked. "Do you like this game?"
"No!" said Sensei. "This is a most stupid game. It calls itself the World Series, yet it is only played by countries that have been dominated by Britain."
He said that most sports were universal, except Cricket; and if you think about it, it is very true.

Sensei Matsuharu Nakazono

Sensei Matsuharu Nakazono started Judo at Tategawa Secondary School in the Kagoshima Province, Japan, and was graded 1st Dan in 1934. He had been promoted to 4th Dan by 1938 and 5th Dan Judo in 1948 (all Kodokan grades).

Prior to studying Judo, however, he had started at 7-years-old, to practice Kendo, and took it up again when in the Army. Hanshi K. Ogawa graded him 3rd Dan Kendo in 1942 at the Butokukwai.

In 1941, Sensei Nakazono studied Aikido under O'Sensei, and by 1956 he had been promoted to 6th Dan.

He represented the Aikikai in Europe and North Africa and was the joint International Chief Instructor of Aikido for the International Budo Council.

Nakazono Sensei's technique was the first seen in the U.K. to both combine the power found with other instructors, with the grace normally associated with Aikido today.

Nakazono Sensei moved to America around 1970.

On Sensei Matsuharu Nakazono:
We had lost all contact with him until I went to teach Aikido in New Mexico USA.

I learned that Nakazono was living in Santa Fe, NM.

After some investigation, he located his telephone number and a meeting was arranged. The meeting with my old teacher was the highlight of my visit to the USA.

I spent four hours with Sensei, who presented me with three books he had written, signing each one of them.

Nakazono Sensei died in 1997 in Santa Fe, NM.

– Henry Ellis, 5th Dan

Sensei Masamichi Norro

Masamichi Norro started Aikido at the Aiki Kai under O'Sensei in April 1954.

He was awarded his 1st Dan in september 1955 and his 2nd Dan in September 1956. By April 1958 he received his 3rd Dan, and in September of the following year, his 4th Dan.

He then became assistant instructor of Aikido at the Aiki Kai Tokyo, and Teacher of the Aikido Section of the Japanese navy. He was awarded his 5th Dan in September 1960.

Sensei Norro came to Europe in August 1961 and became the Official Teacher for the Aiki Kai in Europe and North Africa, together with Sensei Nakazono. He was a resident in France and visited England, Belgium and Africa to teach Aikido.

In January 1963, he was awarded his 6th Dan from the Headquarters of the Aiki Kai, Tokyo. He then became the joint International instructor of Aikido to the International Budo Council.

Sensei Norro was the instructor who introduced the "Forms" system of teaching Aikido to the U.K. - a system still used by the Ellis School, but abandoned by most others.

On Sensei Masamichi Norro:
Norro Sensei made several visits to Britain in the early 1960s to teach at the Hut. We in return, made several visits to his dojo in Paris. It was on one of these visits to Paris with Sensei trevor Jones that Derek Eastman received his second dan from Norro Sensei. Norro Sensei then went into a kind of seclusion for many years. He was now teaching his own style of Aikido. We are pleased to see that he is now to be seen at many of the large European seminars along with the present Doshu.

Norro Sensei at the Hut
in 1961.

Sensei Tadashe Abbe

Sensei Tadashi Abbe studied Aikido under the direct supervision of O'Sensei for a period of nine years.

He travelled to France in 1952 when he was a 6th Dan, as representative of the Aiki Kai Hombu, to be the first Aikido Master in Europe.

Although based in Paris, Sensei Tadashi Abbe visited the UK on several occasions to teach and demonstrate with Sensei Kenshiro Abbe.

Abbe Sensei's technique was hard, fast and powerful.

Tadashi Abbe Sensei was perhaps the hardest of all the teachers ever to graduate from the Aiki-Kai.

On Tadashi Abbe Sensei:
He was perhaps the hardest of all the teachers ever to graduate from the Aiki Kai.
His idea of a good night out, was to be taken to a tough dock area and left for a few hours to test his Aikido against street fighters. He did this in the East Docks of London, but his favorite haunt was the docks of Marseille in France.

He said a man fighting with his fists was no competition, yet if you had empty hands and your opponent has a knife – now that is far more interesting.

Sensei would point out various cuts on his arms, and state where they had taken place. He also said the knife fighters of Marseille were the best he had ever met.

– Henry Ellis, 5th Dan

Sensei Matsutaru Otani

Matsutaru Otani took up Judo in 1917 and studied for two years under Seizo Usui, 2nd Dan, (Kodokan).

Otani came to Britain in 1919 and two years later, joined the Budokwai and studied under Hikoichi Aida. Later, he became an assistant to Yukio Tani, Butokwai Chief Instructor.

Sensei Otani had been fortunate to study under some of the most famous Judo instructors, including: Sensei Kabumoto, Sensei Ishiguro and Sensei Kotani. He was personally graded by Shuichi Nagaoka, 10th Dan (the highest rank in Judo).

Sensei Otani was the instructor for Judo at Oxford University for six years, and Cambridge University for five years. His promotion to 4th Dan came from Yukio Tani, and his 5th Dan from Ichiro Hata.

When Kenshiro Abbe came to England in 1955, Matsutaro Otani followed him and was promoted to 6th Dan. In 1959 he became 7th Dan and National Coach of the British Judo Council, taking over from Abbe Sensei. After a distinguished teaching career, Sensei Otani died in 1977.

Other great teachers

Also visiting and teaching in Britain during the 1960s were: Tada Sensei, 7th Dan; Hishamura Sensei, 4th Dan; and Nobuyoshi Tamura, 7th Dan.

Of these, Tamura Sensei visited the "Hut" to teach on several occasions. He still teaches and practices today. He is considered by many of the original Uchi Deshi of O'Sensei, to be one of the most knowledgeable of all the current Aikido Masters and is based in Paris, France.

The Authors: Sensei Dave Rogers, Sensei Henry Ellis and Sensei Derek Eastman

Henry Ellis was born May 3, 1936 in a tough coal mining area near Rotherham South Yorkshire. United Kingdom. his childhood was hard and deprived as were most kids in those war torn years. His father, a hardened coal miner, handed down to Henry the strict no nonsense Victorian values that he himself had endured at the hands of his own brutal father. Henry knew nothing other than strict discipline in his youth - something which was to stand him in good stead in his later years. He spent two years in a special school for so called "tough kids" which would have made a "juvenile correction facility seem like a Holiday Camp."

Henry was interested in all sports and, at the age of fourteen, joined a cycling club, At 15 he entered his first Time Trial race and won three prizes, finding himself elevated to be the third rider in the club team. This was his passion until starting Judo at the now famous Hut Dojo. It was whilst practising Judo in the 1950's that he saw the "new " martial art of Aikido.

He then gave up both cycling and judo to concentrate solely on Aikido.

At the age of nineteen he was accepted into the newly formed Aikido section at the Hut Dojo. The discipline and etiquette was something that very few students could take and it was now that for the first time he was able to fall back into the strict discipline that was an every-day part of his early life.

Henry found in Aikido something that appealed to his nature. In those early days Aikido was hard and positive - hence the title of this book. Also in those days there was a true "no nonsense" approach to Aikido. This approach is still Henry's focus and he is proud to have been an important part of Aikido's early development within the United Kingdom.

When initially approached to cooperate in this book, he immediately stated that the book must be honest and practical with no references to floating around the planets and other mystical and magical nonsense.

Whilst Henry believe's that the heavy hand of his father shaped his childhood the rest of his life was moulded by his respect for his teacher Kenshiro Abbe Sensei.

Derek Eastman was born 1943 in West London. Although Derek was too young to remember the war, he clearly remembers the difficult post war years and the devastation of London. Even though life was hard, he recalls that he had a happy childhood. His family later moved to the London suburb of Southall where Derek took an interest in all sports, in particular track and field for which he represented both school and county. On leaving school he became an apprentice mechanical engineer, and bought his first motor bike. At the age of sixteen he joined his friends and their "motor bike gang" , they would often visit Windsor and join in the fights with the Queens guards which in those days was the norm.

Derek was very game, but often came off the worse for wear. he decided to toughen himself up and join the Hut Dojo which he had often passed on the road. He visited the Hut and it was here that he met his teacher Henry Ellis. In 1968 Derek had two dojo's and as a member of the Martial Art Commission he needed a name for his dojo's. He approached Henry Ellis and asked if he could use his name for his organisation as Mr Williams had used Abbe sensei's name for the "Abbe School of Budo". Mr Ellis agreed and they joined their schools together to form the "Ellis Schools of Traditional Aikido."

━━━━━━━━━━━━━━━━━━━━━━━━━━━━

Dave Rogers was born in 1966 in Providence, Rhode Island, USA. He grew up in Seekonk, Massachussettes, the proud son of truck driver and former Navy enlisted man, Ed Rogers and his wife, Beverly.

While not sports-oriented, Rogers surprised his parents by joining an American Kenpo Karate class led by Donald Hume in 1980. Upon graduation from High School, he then promptly joined the U.S. Air Force, and was soon stationed at RAF Greenham Common, Berkshire, United Kingdom. It was here Rogers and his long-time friend Al Montemar joined the Basingstoke Aikido Club where they met their teachers, Senseis Henry Ellis, Derek Eastman, Keith Webb and David Warne.

Practices in the 80s with this group were fierce, but the two Americans stayed until the base closed in 1990 with the advent of a treaty with and eventual collapse of the Soviet Union.

Rogers promised to open a club in the U.S., and the first Ellis School in America opened its doors in Alamogordo, NM just a few months into 1990.

Although serving in many different capacities over the years including duty with the 1st Marine Expeditionary Unit in Somalia, 1993; a 5-year stint as a daily newspaper reporter and editor; and several years as a graphic artist for the State of New Mexico, Rogers has always maintained the U.S. branch of the school. In 1999, he finished a manuscript which was originally intended as an informative brochure for the U.S. branch of the Aikido School. In 2000, it became obvious that the brochure was now a book, and Rogers contacted his teachers to ask for their help.

This book, Positive Aikido, is the result.

153

Bracknell Aikido
Club..
Bracknell: Coopers
Hill Youth Centre
Crowthorne Road
North
Bracknell
Royal County of Berk-
shire.
United Kingdom
RG12 7QS

AWRE Aldermarston
Social Club
Tadley Road
Berkshire
United Kingdom
Tuesday 8pm to 9pm

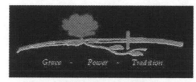

Grace - Power - Tradition

**U.K. Headquarters
for the Ellis Schools
Basingstoke, Hampshire**

**Branch clubs in the U.K. are located
in Bracknell, Frimley and
Aldermaston, United Kingdom.**

For more information, contact:
Sensei Henry Ellis at
ellisaikido@ntlworld.com

Monday 8pm to 9-30pm
Friday   7-30 - 8-30pm

Basingstoke Aikido Club
Basingstoke Sports Centre
Basingstoke Town Centre
Hampshire
United Kingdom
Fri 7-30pm - 9pm

U.S. Headquarters, Ellis Schools

THE HUT
Combat Arts Club

For more information on
the Aikido Program, call
Paul Emel at
paulemel@hotmail.com,
Bill Loose at
Loosebll@wmconnect.com.

**Sun World
Athletic Club
815 9th St.
Alamogordo, NM 88310
The Hut, Alamogordo, was founded in 1990
for the pursuit of Aikido as well as several
other martial arts. The Aikido program
remains active today at Sun World Athletic
Club in Alamogordo, New Mexico. Instruction at this dojo takes place Mondays and
Wednesdays and is provided by Dave
Rogers, 3rd Dan and Paul Emel, 1st Dan
along with Bill Loose, 1st Kyu. Operated by
Chuck Scovone, Sun World is a full-service
gym with a no-nonsense attitude. An exten-
sive collection of fitness machines is augmented by free-weights, tanning booths,
stationary cycles, raquetball courts and two
high-powered martial art programs (Aikido
and Kanjukenbo Karate) as well as boxing.
Call Chuck Scovone at 439-8233
for more information.**

**Texas Branch
Contact Sensei Al Montemar at AlMontemar@loanware.com**

Printed in the United States
by Baker & Taylor Publisher Services